The Sarah Wainwright Story

Extraordinary Episodes from the Life of an Ordinary Woman

Jean Wild

authorHOUSE®

AuthorHouse™ UK Ltd.
500 Avebury Boulevard
Central Milton Keynes, MK9 2BE
www.authorhouse.co.uk
Phone: 08001974150

© 2010 Jean Wild. All rights reserved.

No part of this book may be reproduced, stored in a retrieval system, or transmitted by any means without the written permission of the author.

First published by AuthorHouse 4/7/2010

ISBN: 978-1-4389-8257-1 (sc)

This book is printed on acid-free paper.

This book is dedicated to

My son who shone without me.

Acknowledgements

I am grateful to three women for helping me to realise my ambition to publish this book.

Beth Lister, also a writer, whom I met in my first writing group, has always encouraged me. She was instrumental in persuading me to perform publicly in a play that I wrote in the 80's.

Vanda Inman (www.writespace.com) was the first person to read and edit my work. Thanks to her positivity I've been able to persevere through numerous edits and many crises of confidence.

Dorothy Rowe will never know that her many commonsense and easy to read books have helped me to live my life, emerge from frequent depressions and once to recover from an attempted suicide.

Memory is the seamstress and a capricious one at that. Memory runs her needle in and out and up and down, hither and thither. We know not what comes next, or what follows after.

(Virginia Wolfe, *Orlando*)

Prologue

I sit on Simon's seat when I want to remember. It's under a very old oak tree, which, from a distance, looks almost dead – a bit like me nowadays, I suppose. I have wonderful views from here across the valley to the church of this Brittany village where I now reside and where I hope to live out my days.

I call it 'Simon's seat' although he never sat here, but it is here that I feel closest to him. The oak tree was here before me and will be here long after me. It puts my life into perspective – a life in which I have learned a few things. I am not totally stupid *now*, although I was exceptionally so as a young woman being both ignorant and naïve. To use a cliché, 'hindsight is a wonderful thing'. But things change as well as people, and I did what I did with the information I had at the time. And that is the point of these stories. It is here that I learned to remember and accept myself – my past mistakes, failures and successes. The memories are not all sad, but it is by allowing in the ones that I have for years repressed that I have found a more peaceful existence. If, by the reading, other women can glean some hope or knowledge however slight, then it will be worth the telling.

And that is what I am about to do. I am going to tell you a story about the woman/girl I used to be. It is easy to call her by another name because I am not her now, and she lived in a different world from the one I inhabit today. So here is the story of Sarah Wainwright.

Jean Wild

Introduction to Chapter One

When I first moved here, I was struck by the clothes the Breton people wore. The women dressed in the style of my mother, who died at ninety- three twenty years ago. Crimplene dresses with full wrap-around pinafores seemed to be the uniform. I know crimplene never wears out, but it does become shabby after a few years; yet they all looked so fresh. *Where on earth do they get them?* I wondered. My first visit to the local market enlightened me. Rows and rows of crimplene dresses and wrap-around pinnies hung from almost every stall. Seeing the crimplene dresses was the spark that ignited my memory; I sat on Simon's seat and recalled how he was conceived by that other woman.

Chapter One

The Crimplene Dress

It was ice blue. – Ice blue crimplene. I know what you're thinking: 'Good God, crimplene!' But back then in the early sixties, it was the new miracle fabric. I bought the dress from the village shop for £3. It was a small village, and, like most villages I suppose, everyone knew everyone else; more importantly, we all knew each other's private lives. I can hardly believe my memory now, but we lived in a terraced house which had cost less than £900 – honestly, £900. So you can imagine £3 for a dress was expensive.

The house was primitive compared to today's standards. My husband, Jim, and my dad spent a whole day replacing the big white sink with a white-wood sink unit fitted with a bubbly fibreglass top. It always leaked. I laid vinyl over the uneven, sloping floor. I stuck on a lino wall covering, which was supposed to look like tiles and never really stuck. I also built a wall cupboard out of an old apple box and made work tops from fibre board covered in Fablon. My friend Diane said it looked like a real fitted kitchen. I wasn't convinced, but pretending was something at which I excelled. Anyway, back to the dress.

It had long sleeves, a boat neck, and a tie belt and was really comfortable to wear. I thought how much easier life would be from now on if all our clothes were crimplene. I could just run them through the washer (I was the first person in my street to have an automatic machine bought with my first month's pay as an unqualified teacher), and they would come out almost dry. They wouldn't need ironing. No ironing! It would change my life. And it did in a way, but not the way I expected it to. The events that happened to me when I was wearing that dress affected my whole life and are still doing so.

I also bought a necklace of big shiny pink pearls. That was the same Christmas that I used my 'coop divvy' to buy little treats for everyone; the necklace was my treat. I had never had a Xmas present before. In fact I hadn't had any kind of present or even a card before.

Anyway, this year I had my dress and necklace and a plan. On Christmas Eve, when all the presents were wrapped and the boys were asleep, I would get dressed up. I would take off my old jumper and trousers and have a bath. Next I'd put on my crimplene dress and pearly necklace just for him – not because I was going out or anything but just for him. We would have a drink and watch TV together and then go to bed to make passionate love. I would close my eyes and remember how good it had been before we were married and it all started to go wrong. My plan was sure to please him, and I hoped that he would behave more kindly in future. It couldn't fail.

As I sat eating chocolates, drinking sherry, and watching TV, I thought how surprised and pleased he'd be when he returned from his night in the pub with the lads to find me looking like a model and willing to have sex with him. That part made me feel a little anxious. But I told myself that I could do it. *Dig your fingernails as hard as you can into your palms. That usually works. Just do it to get through Xmas*, I told myself.

He won't be long now, and he'll be so pleased that I waited up, I thought. I concentrated on how good I was looking. I prayed it would all be worthwhile. *We'll still have a lovely Xmas*, I thought. I looked at my watch frequently. As the minutes and the hours ticked away, my mood changed. My mind raced. *How dare he stay out so late on Xmas Eve? I thought he had more consideration for the boys, if not for me. If I go to bed now, he'll never know about my plan. It will all be a waste of time and effort.* But I knew how he dared. I remembered the early days of our courtship and marriage. I suppose you'd call it a 'relationship' these days.

He was the handsomest lad in town. And the funniest. He was the best dressed too. He wore cavalry twill trousers and a Harris Tweed sports jacket. His important-looking tie lay on his immaculately ironed white shirt, which was always spotless. All the girls wanted him, and I was no exception. The latest and most daring hairstyle for young men at the time was the crew cut, and he had the shortest. He was taller than me, and his short hair made his dark-brown eyes seem deep and unfathomable. He only had to look down at me with those eyes, and my knees would turn to jelly. I could barely speak to him because my mouth wouldn't work in his presence. So when he let it be known that he fancied me, through a friend of course, I turned up at the suggested time and place. We often went to the pictures and, in the summer, for walks, but he wasn't reliable and dated other girls. Why I was so stupid I have no idea. Even writing this I cannot believe how brainless I was. But you have to remember *The Female Eunuch* would not have been written, and I would not have known what a consciousness-raising group for women was even if I'd been semi-conscious. I was a Stepford girlfriend.

Why had I married him? I was supposed to be intelligent. I could write essays and pass exams. I was in the second year of a two-year teachers' training course when I became pregnant. Jim was in the army but had spent a weekend in my college pretending to be a new student – mostly in my room and in my bed to be precise. He was due to be sent to Germany. I expect that made us reckless. I remember enjoying the kissing but not the sex. Why did I do it? I have no idea. The only 'excuse' or 'reason' I can offer is that as well as being incredibly stupid I was scared of hurting his feelings by saying no. It never entered my head that I would get pregnant. Like I say, I was stupid with a capital S.

Maggie, my best friend in college, came with me to a doctor in town because I was too afraid to go to the college doctor. I don't know what I thought he could do to me.

'Now then,' he said, 'you will have to tell the principal of your condition. I suggest you write a letter to her saying that you find that you are three months pregnant.'

'Will you prescribe a tonic for her, Doctor? She seems to be a bit rundown,' Maggie said.

And he did. I felt about twelve, certainly not old enough to become a parent. Now my mother's hopes for her clever daughter becoming a teacher were truly dashed; instead, I was going to become a mother.

I wrote the note to the principal and was duly called to her private flat.

'Well, Miss Williams, tell me more about your situation. When is your baby due?'

'In June,' I whispered, feeling like the world's greatest sinner.

'Pity,' she said. 'Had it been later, July even, you could have stayed and taken your finals.'

That comment did little to assuage the guilt. Academia may look on these things more liberally, but my village wouldn't and my mother certainly would not.

'I don't know how you are going to tell your mother,' Maggie said.

'Nor do I. But I have to.'

In the event, I didn't have to. I went home one weekend to break the news. I was standing in front of the fireplace trying to compose a sentence.

'I have to tell you...'

'You are pregnant,' said my mother, who knew me, it seemed, better than I knew myself.

And that was that. I left college one weekday when all my friends were in lectures. My father came to collect me in his car. Poor Dad. He must have felt more ashamed than me if that was possible. I would have happily turned into a snake and wriggled away through the grass. No one waved me good-bye. There was no leaving party, and I felt like a criminal. We drove home in silence – I could say 'pregnant silence' but that would be making light of a situation that felt worse than death.

So that's why I had married him. I was pregnant.

He came back from Germany for two weeks for the wedding and the 'honeymoon'.

If only I'd known what a frightened human being he was except when he was bullying me. He was a Jekyll and Hyde character. I thought he was so confident and adult, always the life and soul of the party before we were married. But after, I found out that it was all a façade to cover his real character. He didn't even tell the army that he was married and that I was expecting a baby. If my mum and dad hadn't allowed me to stay with them, how would I have lived? They were devastated that I had to leave college. They had been so proud when they thought that I was going to be a teacher.

I survived by buying a knitting machine on HP, thanks to my dad's signature. I spent every back-breaking hour knitting to help pay for my keep. And I managed to get temporary part-time work in a factory until the delivery.

A friend told me about SSAFFA (Soldiers, Sailors and Air Force Family Association). This turned out to be a very kind elderly lady living in a tiny cottage.

'You have every right to have an allowance.'

I was too scared to even lift my head up in the street because I was pregnant before marriage. But she never even referred to that.

'And when the baby is born, you will get an increase for the baby. Write to his CO. Tell him everything and address it to the commanding officer at the same address that you write to your husband. What's wrong with these young men that they can't take responsibility?'

My mother-in-law said, 'You'll have to do it, Sally. He won't. He's too scared, you know.'

I didn't know, but I was about to find out that he was scared of his own shadow, but not of me. So I wrote, and I even got back pay from the date of our wedding.

Not only was he not pleased about this, he was bloody furious. That's when I started to lose respect for him, and he started to hate me. By the time he was demobbed, there was no love left on either side.

I remember when he finally came home from Germany. It was in the middle of the night. He threw stones up at the window so as to waken me but not my parents. I crept downstairs and opened the front door. There he was, and all I felt was his prickly army uniform. But I was married to him. My feelings terrified me. How could I ever trust myself again? I pushed all these thoughts to the back of my mind. I subdued my feelings. The reality was too scary to contemplate. I was married to this man. He was the father of my child. We had to spend the rest of our lives together. The law said so, the church said so, and so did my family and friends and, most important of all, my mother.

So here I was trying to 'make it work' but really dying inside. The evening dragged as I watched programme after programme and he didn't come home. I quelled my worries by thinking that he would stay out until closing time. Closing time came and went. I changed channels as each one closed down.

Please stay on. It's Xmas Eve. You broadcast really late on Xmas Eve. Everyone stays up late tonight.

Even after the TV had emitted its final signal and broke my reverie, I remained hopeful. I tried to read. Reading had become my means of survival. I could escape to other worlds away from the nightmare of nappies and housework. Looking back I realise that most of the books I read had poor role models. All the heroines seemed to have to 'get their man' to succeed. Sitting without the TV reminded me how important the TV was to him and how important staying married was to my mother.

The year before, our rental set had broken down.

'So what will you say when you ring up?' he had said. 'Tell them we want it repaired straight away. We pay enough bleeding rent. They should bring another set. I don't want to miss the match on Saturday. Now tell me again. What will you say? Tell them about the match. It's a crap TV anyway. They should have brought a better one. Are you sure you've paid? It's just like you to have missed. Tell me again what will you say?'

On and on he went till I couldn't think. Bear in mind that we had no telephone and I had to take two toddlers (oh yes, I'd had another baby by then) to a phone box which was at the top of a hill. So I made the phone call, and when he came home from work I walked out and went to my mother's. I had left the children in bed. I knew he wouldn't leave them alone in the house.

'I've come to stay here until the TV is repaired,' I said. 'Jim acts like a madman when we have no TV.'

I didn't tell her that he used it to 'gas light' me also. I would sit with him sometimes watching a film and become interested in it. If I went out of the room or even looked away, he would change channels surreptitiously. I'd make comments like 'who's he' and 'how does he fit into the story'. Then he would change back again without my noticing. After it happened a few times I'd say, 'I can't follow this', and leave the room. It was a few years before I realised what he was doing. Of course he denied it. When your confidence is slowly chipped away, you always believe other people.

On this occasion my mother woke me at six o'clock the next morning.

'Come on. Get off home now. Go and get Jim's breakfast. You don't want him to be late for work, do you?'

What went on behind the front door was irrelevant as long as we were both inside.

On and on ran my thoughts as on and on ticked the clock.

OK, I thought, *I'll show him what he's missed, and I'll show him that he can't treat me like this anymore. Things will have to change. He's got to come soon. He can't stay out all night. I have to stay awake. I mustn't get drunk.*

But the plan was ruined. The clock said five o'clock. I realized that the kids would soon be awake.

'What a bloody stupid thing I've done! Now I'm so tired I won't be able to enjoy Xmas Day with them. Christ, I hate him,' I said out loud as I dragged myself upstairs. 'How am I ever going to escape from this mind-numbingly boring nightmare? Can it be real?'

I dropped the crimplene dress on the floor and crawled into bed. I fell asleep wondering what had happened to the plans I had made in college with Kate and Maggie. I should be in Canada now. Not living the life of a terrified drudge pretending to like housework and looking after babies. When the excited boys woke me, he was in bed beside me. I dared to shake him awake.

'Please get up to watch the boys. Open their presents.'

Surprisingly he sat up, put on his slippers and dressing gown, and followed them downstairs.

He's either feeling very guilty or he's still drunk, I thought. But there were no excuses or explanations and certainly no apologies.

Back to normal then, I thought as he returned to bed after the present opening and I dragged myself into the kitchen to prepare the Xmas dinner.

****

A year passed, and life continued in the same vein except that I tried to look for escape routes. By the following Xmas I thought I had found one.

'That's the colour I would have chosen for you,' said Nick as he passed me a plate of sandwiches to take into the dining room.

'What?'

'If I had bought a dress for you, that's the colour I would have chosen.'

Our eyes met, but I looked down immediately at the dress and remembered how I had felt last Xmas when I had first worn it. Today all I felt was cold.

I had met Nick at a public meeting when trying to get away from the mind numbingly boring life of housewife and mother. There is only so much time one can be interested in a newly fitted carpet and a teak dining-room suite. Also, counting games and nursery rhymes had long since lost their novelty. A campaign for a town swimming pool had been started. As Jim was away during the week training to be a fireman, I found a friendly neighbour to baby-sit whilst I went to the meetings. It was my first taste of politics. I was too afraid to open my mouth at first but soon began to chip in my twopen'th. Nick really impressed me from the start by standing up in a full Town Hall and speaking out confidently. How different he was from Jim who had only two interests in life. One was being cruel to me and the other was football. He trained two nights a week, played a match on Saturday afternoon, watched *Match of the Day* Saturday evening, and played in the Sunday league on Sunday morning. Sunday afternoons were spent at his mother's watching *Match of the Day* a second time.

So I began to go to council meetings with Nick, and he would walk me home. Neither of us could drive. He always left me at the door. I wasn't physically attracted to him. He wasn't a handsome man – not like Jim – but he listened to me when I spoke and seemed interested in my ideas. His horn-rimmed specs and untidy appearance did not seem to matter. I began to see a more interesting world in which people talked of things other than nappies and housework. His confident manner and intelligent conversation became more important than his lack of looks and dress sense. What was more exciting was that I thought I saw a glimmer of light at the end of a long tunnel. Then at Xmas we were invited to a friend's house for a tea party for adults and children. There was no central heating, and the kitchen and dining room were fridge-like. My dress had long sleeves and felt thick. One would have thought that it would be warm to wear, but not crimplene, not ice-blue crimplene. I shivered as I took the sandwiches and placed them on the table, which was heaving with Xmas fare.

Nick noticed me shiver and placed his hand on my shoulder, saying, 'Why don't you go and sit by the fire in the other room? I've sent your boys upstairs to play with the other children. There's a fire in the bedroom, and they can play bouncing on the bed.' He paused and added, 'It really suits you, that colour. I wish I'd bought it for you.'

I could still feel his warm hand on my cold shoulder as I sat down in front of the roaring fire. My face glowed from the feelings Nick had stirred in me with that touch, and I turned to look into his eyes. I knew then that although he wasn't as handsome as Jim, I was attracted to him for other reasons. Where had falling for a handsome man got me?

Just then the kids burst into the room, their faces shining and sweaty with the activity. They were noisy and boisterous too because, bed bouncing over, they were bored.

'Come on, kids, into the dining room. Tea's ready. You lot can have your teas first while we grown-ups have a bit of peace by the fire,' a voice called from the hallway.

It was Gill, Nick's wife. Their son ran into the dining room with the other children. I settled back in the armchair to listen to the music. Someone had put on a record and handed me a few others to choose the next. I almost let the pile of 78s fall as Nick leaned over the back of my chair; I felt his breath on my neck.

'I hope that's not how you are feeling now,' he said, indicating the record on top.

'I'm in the Mood for Love,' the label read.

Later I managed to sit at the opposite end of the table from him. I was afraid that someone else would notice the attention he was giving me. And I wasn't at all sure that I wanted to go down this route.

'Would you like more tea?' I heard his voice behind me. My hand shook as I raised my fork. 'Are you still cold? I notice you are shivering.'

I steadied my hand on the edge of the table hoping that no one else had noticed. Leaving the table after the meal, I said, 'Thank you so much for a lovely meal, but we really must get those boys to bed. They've had so many late nights lately.'

I needed to get away so that I could think about what was happening to me. The journey home was dreamlike. It had snowed heavily all afternoon, and it was still snowing gently. The silence was eerie. My stomach lurched when the car slid sideways and we descended the hill.

I've felt enough today to last a whole year. I tried not to think of the future.

****

Jim left for work that Xmas Eve saying he'd be late home. 'We're all going to the Millstone to celebrate.'

I thought, *you're my millstone. I wish I had something to celebrate.*

Nick had asked me to meet him in town, but I had thought it would be too dangerous. Now I changed my mind. If Jim could celebrate, then so could I.

As I fought my way up and down the aisles of the department store, I was unaware of the over-the-top Xmas decorations. Neither did I hear the corny Xmas music, which was so loud it made the speakers buzz. I was only conscious of my own inner turmoil as I looked furtively to left and right trying to see without being seen. Finally I gave up on Nick and bought far too many presents and even a Xmas tree, which I had to carry home on an overcrowded bus. Why had I agreed to come, I wondered, as the bus took forever in the traffic. It was dangerous; there was no point. But I knew why. I was imagining a future. Sally and Nick. Nick and Sally. It sounded right. It felt right. We should be together. He had given me a Xmas present. When I opened the packet, the sight of the bottle of Chanel No. 5 took my breath away. It was the first bottle of perfume I'd ever had. It wasn't just a present, was it? It was like giving the moon and stars. I said before that I was stupid. I think this proves it.

Next time we met I said, 'I waited ages.'

'So did I,' he said. 'We must have just missed each other. It was so crowded.'

I believed him. How could I not? He had given me the moon and stars.

It wasn't just the flattery and attention I enjoyed. It was our shared interest in politics, which was so much better than boring football. Jim was away one week on a course. It was too easy. Nick called one evening when the children were in bed.

As we sat before the fire my face glowed – and it was not just the glow from the fire. We passionately discussed our political ideas, but he was also holding my hand.

'I think council houses are a good idea,' I said. 'The trouble is there just aren't enough. And there is too much corruption. People jump the list. It's not how needy you are; it's who you know that gets you a house.'

'You're right of course,' he said, turning to face me. 'But just now, I think that this is the most beautiful music I've ever heard,' he said, referring to the Bruch violin concerto which was playing. 'And your face is the most beautiful I've ever seen. Now I'm going to do this.'

He grabbed me and kissed me, and somehow we were no longer sitting in front of the fire holding hands. I was lying on the carpet feeling the full weight of him on top of me. I struggled a little as he raised my crimplene dress and eased down my stockings. Not really wanting this. Not feeling, not feeling, not feeling anything. I was dazed. He placed a finger on my forehead, saying, 'Just relax.' And I did. I drifted into a kind of trance, thinking, *He loves me. Everything is going to change.* I saw that light drawing nearer. Don't forget I was really naïve.

I was jolted back to reality when he withdrew and ejaculated on my stomach. So soon that light began to dim.

'I don't think much of your method of contraception,' I said.

'I'm really sorry. But I get so excited when I'm with you, I can't control myself. I couldn't help it.'

We never had sex again, for that's what it was – not love as I'd deceived myself into thinking. I knew almost immediately that I was pregnant.

'Yes, I am sure,' I said when he asked.

'Well, what do you expect me to do? I never made you any promises. I never talked about the future. If we meet again in forty years time, we will relate in exactly the same way. We have the same values, and the chemistry will always be there.'

I couldn't speak. It was true that he hadn't made any promises or talked about the future. He said he had a friend who was a chemist, and he would ask him for some tablets. A few days later he handed me two tablets and said, 'I'm not sure that they will work now because it is too late. But you can try.'

Of course they didn't 'work'. I thought that they looked like aspirin. How could I have been such a fool? I had to do something myself. So I went to the doctor's.

'I'm pregnant,' I told the doctor.

'That is for me to tell you,' said the doctor.

I stifled the words, 'I'm fairly sure I know my own body', and said instead, 'I've missed two periods, my breasts are tender, and I have to pee frequently.'

After an internal examination he said, 'You are three months pregnant.'

Bloody men, I thought. *Why do they have to control us?* The light was gone. The tunnel didn't even exist now. I was well and truly trapped. What I'd seen as an escape route had turned out to be a ball and chain to keep me prisoner. I tensed myself and said with a confidence I didn't feel, 'I want to have this baby adopted.'

'Now then, my dear, you are going to have this child, and you will love it just as you love your other children.'

I decided that there would be no point trying to argue with the doctor, so I left the surgery. As soon as I reached the street I darted into an empty bus shelter and sobbed and sobbed.

The next time I saw Nick, he greeted me with, 'I've got details of a Mother-and-Baby home you can go to. It's easy. You can stay there for six months. They will take the baby away after it is born and put it up for adoption. And that will be that.'

'Put it up for adoption! You talk as though it's a piece of furniture in an auction. Put it up? You are talking about a life, your own child's life. That will be that? Is that what you think? If I never see my child again, I'll forget? You may be able to do that, but I can't.'

'It seems to be the simplest of solutions to me.'

'It is simple, for you. What the hell do you think I am going to do with the boys? What do I tell my family? Just go. How could I ever have thought I loved you? I must have been mad. Go. Get out. Just leave me alone.'

But I did see him again. I was walking home from shopping when I saw him on the other side of the road. He was with another woman. A few months later, I saw the other woman in the super market. She was very pregnant. I wondered if Nick's wife ever found out about his affairs.

Do some men have a laser device that shuts off women's brains?

One day I was ironing wearing the crimplene dress, which had now been relegated to a working frock. Jim was reading the paper.

He said, 'You know last night when you said that it didn't matter about a Durex?'

I nodded.

'And I said, "What do you want this time, a girl or a boy?"'

I couldn't answer.

I pressed down hard on the shirt I was ironing. I couldn't see the shirt for the tears were blinding me.

'It's not mine, is it?'

I shook my head.

'Well, who the bloody hell's is it then?'

The tears oozed out and rained down my face onto the shirt. I watched as the iron slid over them and they disappeared. More fell, and I ironed them away too. I didn't answer. Couldn't answer.

'It's that bugger. Christ, I didn't believe it when they told me he'd been seen coming out of this house when I was away. I bloody well trusted you, you bitch! I've been a good husband to you, and this is how you repay me.'

I knew I was in the wrong. There was no denying that, but if I hadn't been crying so hard, I might have laughed at the 'good husband' bit.

Jim's sister arrived early one morning. She sat and smoked a cigarette and totally ignored me while she waited for him to get ready. They left the house together without saying where they were going. It was a weekday, so they must have gone somewhere important to both have taken time off work. He returned alone a couple of hours later, all cocky and jeering.

'Well, that's it. I can chuck you out and change the locks and keep the kids, and there's not a thing you can do about it.'

He sat smirking.

'How are you going to look after the boys and go to work?' I said. 'They don't even go to school yet.'

'We'll work something out. My mother will help. She's disgusted with you and what you've done.'

****

On a warm autumn day I was halfway to my parent's house, dripping with sweat and breast milk in the shapeless crimplene dress. That day I learned the true qualities of crimplene. More importantly, I learned that swapping one man for another doesn't work. It just makes things worse, much worse, especially if the man in question is married. It was too late now to heed the warning, 'Beware of men bearing expensive gifts'. The leaves were all the colours that poets and artists go into raptures about. I was feeling the exact opposite of rapturous. I dragged one foot after the other wondering if the agony would ever end. The scenes of the past year played like a film in my mind as I plodded on.

The kind lady from the adoption society, who happened to be a vicar's wife, had come to visit before and after the adoption. I had sarcastically nicknamed her Mrs Angel. Jim was there at the 'before' meeting. Apparently he had to be.

'Now then, you two,' Mrs Angel had said, 'why do you think your marriage has gone wrong? You are still very young.'

'That's it,' Jim said. 'She was too young, too immature. Not ready for marriage.'

'Rubbish. Who has taken all the responsibilities? Me. Who pays the bills? Me. Who does everything – housework, gardening, decorating, child care? Me. *And* I go to work. What do *you* do? Play football!'

I surprised myself daring to say these things in front of him, and I knew it was a case of speak now pay later.

'Well, that's cleared things up. I'm sure you'll work things out now and get on with each other a little better.'

Is she for real? I thought. *Was that supposed to be marriage guidance counselling? Christ, you don't live in the same world as us.*

The 'after' meeting was much worse. I was alone when Mrs Angel came to tell me what a wonderful family my son had gone to. She was not big on tact.

'My baby was born with webbed feet,' I ventured.

I hadn't even spoken the words 'my baby' to anyone before. The subject was strictly taboo. It was 'madness making' just having to talk to the very woman who had arranged for my baby to be taken away.

'Oh yes. His father noticed and laughed. He said he would be a good swimmer.'

'Maybe when he grows up, he will come and find me.'

Mrs Angel looked down. 'Yes, maybe.'

She knew full well that neither party was allowed by law to have any knowledge of the other, ever. Of course this information was not imparted to me.

I remembered the registrar in the hospital. I had sat in a long narrow room feeling like Alice after taking the shrinking potion.

'Name?' said the registrar from behind the enormous desk at the other end, pen poised over the register.

'Simon.'

'Mother's name?'

'Sarah Wainwright.'

'Father's name?'

I hesitated then stuttered, 'Nick... er... Nicholas Moore.'

'What?'

I repeated it.

'You are not married to the father? Then I don't need his name.'

Bastard, I thought, meaning the registrar, not my child. I didn't see the irony at the time.

I remembered June, a colleague, had come to visit soon after the birth:

'So what happened? Where's the baby? In bed?'

'The baby died. It was a boy. Stillborn.'

A voice from somewhere had lied. It couldn't have been my voice. I couldn't have lied about my own child.

'You know what everyone's saying? They're saying—'

'Yes, well, it's not true,' the voice lied again.

'That's awful. You must stop the rumours. If it was me, I'd put a notice in the paper. I'd—'

'I don't care what they say. I've lost my baby,' the voice said truthfully.

June left.

I climbed the hill to my parent's house; tears were streaming down my face and joining the rivers of sweat and milk. *I'm turning to liquid*, I thought. *It's got to stop*. I opened the front door and ran straight to the bathroom. I washed away the sweat, tears, and milk. I slipped the fated crimplene dress on again, gritted my teeth, closed my memory like an iron trap, ran downstairs into the living room, sat down, and lit a cigarette.

Then for some reason unknown to God or man my father said, 'Smile. I've got a new camera.'

He took a photograph of me, which he later framed and placed on the TV. Of course I was wearing that bloody dress.

Some weeks later we were spending the evening in the usual way:

James lying full length on the settee watching TV and me alternating between knitting and reading.

'Stop clacking those bloody needles. You sit there as though nothing has happened. And that book. Give it here. I'll burn the bloody thing.'

I didn't respond. I just sat there motionless. Numb.

'Think yourself lucky I didn't throw you out. Everybody thinks I'm a fool for letting you stay. In fact I can still throw you out. Go, go, go now. Get out. I don't want you. Nobody wants you. Just looking at you makes me want to puke.'

He wrenched me out of the chair and pushed me towards the door still ranting. I couldn't react. I couldn't feel. I was like a rag doll. He opened the door, threw me into the rainy night, and slammed the door shut. I stood there statue-like, the rain mixing with my tears. Only the thought of leaving the boys kept me standing there. How could I go and leave my two sons? Where could I go? He was right. Nobody wanted me. I didn't even want myself. What did I have to look forward to? A life of shame. Everybody knew what I'd done. Then the door opened, and he dragged me back in.

'What are you standing out there for in the pouring rain? Are you mad? Nobody in their right mind would do that. Now fuck off to bed.'

Obeying his orders I crawled upstairs knowing full well what waited for me as he stamped behind.

'Go on, be quick. Move it.'

Once in bed I knew the routine.

'Right, bitch. You're my wife, and I can fuck you whenever I want. It's the law see. I know my rights. There's nothing you can do to stop me.'

There didn't seem to be any point in trying to stop him. He was right. And what I had done was wrong. Very wrong. Everybody said so. I deserved to be punished.

Evenings began peacefully for him. For me it was torture waiting for the preliminaries. One night when the boys were staying over at my mother's, he beat me up really badly. You'd know if you'd ever been beaten that it only has to happen once. Once beaten, always obedient.

The night of the beating he took the long part of the kids' reins and stretched it out in front of my face. It was made of nylon webbing with metal rings at the end.

'Do you think this will do?'

'What for?'

'For your punishment. You deserve to be whipped within an inch of your life, and I'm going to do it.'

Before I could move he caught me sharply across the face. Then as I turned to run, he grabbed my arm and whipped my legs over and over. I managed to break free, run upstairs, and lock myself in the bathroom.

I'm safe, I thought. Just then I heard a loud bang, and the door burst open. He pinned me up against the wall and just flogged and flogged. Arms, legs, face, all exposed flesh. The metal rings stung, and I screamed with pain. Somehow I managed to wedge myself in the airing cupboard between the wall and the hot-water tank. He couldn't reach me. I screamed for help.

I was just feeling safe when cold water splashed over my head and ran down my neck. But cold water didn't hurt. I could stand that. Then the scalding water reached me. He was pouring scalding hot water over me. I came out of the airing cupboard.

'You stupid bitch. Thought you could get away from me, did you? Now bed. And stop whimpering, or you'll get some more.'

Sometimes he played the poker in the fire game. The first time he played it we were sitting as usual: him sprawled full-length watching the TV, me in the armchair not daring now to read or knit or even move but pretending to watch. He put the poker in the fire and left it there for a few minutes. Then he took it out and said, 'No it's not hot enough yet', and put it back in the fire. He repeated this a few times then said, 'Do you know why I am doing this?'

'No,' I said, genuinely puzzled.

'When it's red hot, I'm going to use it to mark your face. I'm going to brand you so that everybody will know you for what you are. You are wicked and evil and a fornicating bitch and everybody is going to know it by the mark I'm going to put on your face.'

I sat statue-like, palms sticky with sweat, throat dry with fear, and tongue stuck to the roof of my mouth.

Every time he played this game, he'd push the poker towards me saying, 'Do you think it's hot enough yet?'

Speechless, my eyes would widen with fear. Then bringing the poker nearer, he'd say, 'Yes, I think that will do.'

I'd close my eyes, hardly breathing now but feeling the heat of the poker on my cheek. I was rigid, knowing that if I moved a fraction, the searing pain of the red-hot poker would scar my face. Only when I felt the heat move away did I open my eyes.

One night he held the poker so close to my arm I could feel the heat through my dress. Then he moved it even closer and touched the sleeve. Being crimplene it did not burn. It melted.

I never wore the crimplene dress again. But then, there is the photo my father took of me that autumn day, sitting in front of the TV smoking a cigarette.

I look at it sometimes and think, *I'm glad I learned to forget.*

> As the hand held before the eye
> conceals the greatest mountain,
> so the little earthly life hides
> from the glance the enormous lights
> and mysteries of which the world is full,
> and he who can draw it away from before his eyes
> as one draws away the hand,
> beholds the great shining of the inner worlds.
>
> (Rabbi Nachmann of Bratzlav)

Chapter Two
The Break-away

'Three should be enough,' Sarah thought as she put the new bottle of Valium into her handbag and dropped it on the floor. She pulled the covers over her head and snuggled back into the womb of warmth.

'I'll wait until they've all left the house.' And although her eyes were closed, she strained to make out every sound which betrayed the movements of her family downstairs.

At last the front door banged for the third time, and she knew that her husband and two sons had left the house. As she was waiting to make sure that they would be safely in school and work she contemplated her plan. She took the bottle of Valium, unscrewed the top, and tipped a handful of the white pills onto her palm. She stared at them.

'I don't *really* want to die. Life can be good—'

But yours isn't, is it? said her inner voice.

'No, it isn't.'

So what's wrong, then?

'You know what's wrong. It's him. I wish he didn't exist. I wish he would disappear.'

You could murder him.

'Don't be stupid. Knowing my luck, I'd get caught, and even if I didn't, I would spend the rest of my life feeling scared and guilty. That would be worse.'

OK, so you can't kill yourself and you can't kill him.

'You're right. But I am going to do something.'

Yes, but what?

'I'll leave. Now. Today. I'll go as far away as I can, get a job, and stay away. For good, I mean.'

Sarah smiled to herself. She jumped out of bed, ran to the bathroom, flushed the tablets down the loo, showered quickly, and pulled on a pair of jeans and a tee shirt. How stupid to think of committing suicide when there was so much to live for! She thought of all the things she wanted to do, reading, painting, and playing music, but couldn't because they annoyed him. And when he was annoyed – well, she didn't want to dwell on that. *But if I leave, I can do anything I like,* she thought. She picked up a wet towel from the bathroom floor. The boys! She had to make sure that they understood.

She wrote two notes, carefully explaining that she had to leave them although she did love them very much. It was not their fault, the note said, and they must not worry about her. She would be happier alone, and she wanted them to be happier in a household free from domestic violence and abuse. She put a note under each of her son's pillows and went downstairs. In the hall she hesitated for a moment. Would they really be better without her? Would he turn his anger on them? No, they were teenagers now. He never hit them before, why would he start now? Besides, they were bigger than their father. They could take care of themselves.

As she opened the front door she noticed her fiddle case, which lay in the corner. She had played as a child and a couple of years ago she had bought a cheap violin and taken a couple of lessons. Her teacher said she would be good if only she practised more. But her husband had ridiculed her so much that she could only practise when he was out. One day, when she had annoyed him more than usual, he had taken the fiddle from its case and slowly, right in front of her, wound the tuning pegs one by one, tighter and tighter, until they snapped. Well, today she was the one who had snapped. She could take it with her. New strings would be easy to fit. But no, it would be too cumbersome. She sighed and went out, slamming the front door hard behind her.

It was a sunny autumn day. She walked quickly; she could hardly stop herself from running. After drawing as much money as she could from the bank and the building society, she went to the railway station, where she bought a ticket to Crewe. This was quite clever, she thought, because the man in the ticket office at her local station knew her by sight and would be sure to remember if she'd asked for any other destination. At Crewe she could buy a ticket for anywhere in the British Isles.

Yesterday, she had looked at a map in the garage whilst she was waiting for the exhaust to be repaired. She had noticed that Inverness was the northern-most railway station in Scotland. She remembered the map now.

'Single to Inverness, please,' Sarah said and peeled off thirty pounds from the roll of notes in her purse.

There was an hour to wait for the next train, and it would be a long journey. She walked out of the station and found a clothes shop where she enjoyed buying a thick zip-up cardigan with comfy pockets, and she didn't worry about the cost. As she walked back to the station she controlled her urge to run. She must not draw attention to herself. So she sauntered showing a calmness that she didn't feel. She feared being recognised; she would be happier when she was on the train speeding away.

On the train, she wished she had brought a book, for it was a long journey, but there was a restaurant car and for once, she had money. It was restful looking through the window at the scenery and God knows, she needed a rest.

When the train arrived at Inverness, it was dark, chilly, and raining. Standing in the taxi queue, she panicked. She had no idea where to go. She got nearer the front. 'Oh God, what if the taxi driver is unscrupulous. Her could take me anywhere, rape me, and dump me—'

'Next.'

'Can you take me to a bed and breakfast place, please?' Sarah heard herself say as she climbed into the steamed-up taxi.

They seemed to drive in circles, but she couldn't see through the misted windows, and anyway, how would she know? She'd never been to Inverness before.

The taxi stopped and the driver jumped out, saying, 'Wait here, I'll just check for you.' He went to the front door of a corner house in a quiet cul-de-sac. A middle-aged woman with grey hair, wearing an apron and a big smile, stood on the step, nodding.

Once inside, Sarah was so relieved that she felt like sitting on her knee and crying into her neck. Instead, she talked politely about breakfast times, and then went straight to bed.

Sarah had two fears besides her husband. Boredom and sleeplessness. She solved the latter with a tablet. Tomorrow she would solve the other. She drifted off to sleep.

For the next week the skies were clear and the autumn sun warmed the days, but the cloudless skies led to cold evenings. Sarah spent the first couple of days enjoying a freedom that she could not remember ever having experienced before in her entire life.

There was nobody, but nobody, to argue. No 'Don't do this' or 'You can't do that'. Nobody to ask ad nauseam, 'What time will you be back?' She heard the game in her head that he played every time she went out.

'Well, you must have some idea.'

'No I don't.'

'Well, just give me a clue.'

'I have absolutely no idea.'

'But you must know how long the meeting will take.'

'No I don't.'

'Well, have a guess.'

'Honestly, I have no idea.'

'Of course you do, tell me what time you will be back.'

With every question his voice got angrier, and she was afraid that he would stop her from going altogether so she said a time, which was exactly what he wanted her to do. As soon as the words were out of her mouth, she knew it was a mistake; she realised he'd done it again, because if she wasn't home by that exact time, she would suffer for it. It would start again.

'You said you'd be back at ten o'clock.'

'Why did you tell me ten o'clock?'

'You had no intention of coming back at ten, did you?'

'It was a lie, wasn't it?'

'Where have you been till now?'

Now *she* was repeating ad nauseam, 'Wow, what a relief, what a wonderful feeling. Freedom.' As she went in cafés, browsed in shops, and walked by the river, she breathed in deeply and sighed often. She even indulged her passion for the theatre. *This is much better than committing suicide*, she thought.

What luxury, choosing trousers, sweaters, and nighties. She took her time and wallowed in this rare pastime. Sarah was still careful with her money, partly out of habit and partly from necessity. She bought just enough garments at just the right price. Her money would have to last until she found a job. It would be foolish to run out and have to go back.

Having spent her life behind a shyness that had silenced her in the presence of others, she was surprised to discover herself talking easily to the landlady and all the guests. It seemed that the place to visit was the Outer Hebrides. That was if she was a tourist, of course. She thought that perhaps she could be defined as a missing person, but she allowed the other guests to believe that she was a tourist. It wasn't difficult, and no one asked awkward questions.

The Outer Hebrides. It sounded wonderful. It was half a day's train journey and a short ferry ride away. So with her new rucksack packed with new clothes, Sarah made her way to the railway station. This time she bought a ticket to the Kyle of Localsh.

It was a train journey she would never forget, ever. Nothing unusual happened, but for Sarah now every minute was unusual. The sights she beheld through the window were spectacular and breathtaking. She knew that if she travelled the world over, nothing, but nothing, could be more memorable. Of course she had seen postcards of Scotland, of lochs and mountains. She had seen films and oil paintings and photographs, but still she was not prepared for the reality. No word or image had prepared her for the feeling that she experienced on that journey. The scenery was thrilling; it was exciting; it was stimulating. Her stomach shook and wobbled. Her heart beat faster. She wanted to dance and sing and shout in response to the snow-capped mountains. She leaned out of the train window till her neck almost broke to see the snowy peaks. As she stepped off the train onto the platform at Kyle of Lochalsh her knees felt weak and her steps were a little shaky. The journey had been intoxicating. She felt like a different person.

The ferry across to Skye was short, and she knew that she must quickly find somewhere to stay before dark. She saw a house with a bed and breakfast sign and was shown into a freezing cold room. She left her rucksack and joined the family in their living room. There was a roaring fire and a television. As she watched the news she wondered if there would be anything about her. After all she was a missing person. But the world seemed to be carrying on as usual totally unaware of her disappearance. Little did she know that back home the opposite was in fact the case.

When she hadn't come home that first night, her husband Jim had phoned all her friends and family. The boys had kept quiet about their letters. The second day he went to the police and reported her missing. A missing person's report appeared in the local paper. He stopped going to work. On the third day he answered the doorbell to find two uniformed police.

'Mr Wainwright? How do you do, sir? PC Smith and WPC Jones. You reported your wife missing a few days ago?'

'Have you found her? Is she OK?'

'May we come in, sir? We really don't want to talk on the doorstep.'

Jim showed them into the sitting room. The policewoman sat in an armchair and suggested he do the same, but PC Smith walked around the room picking up ornaments and looking at photos.

'Is this her, sir, your wife?' he said, picking up a photo which stood on the TV.

'Yes, yes. It's the same one I gave in at the station when I reported her missing. Have you found her?'

'Good-looking woman. You must be really proud to be seen out with her.'

'What's that supposed to mean? What are you saying?'

'Other men looked at her when you were out, did they? Made you jealous, did they?'

'What in the name of God has all this to do with anything? She's been gone for three days now, and you waste your time making stupid comments like that. Why aren't you out there looking for her?'

PC Smith put the photo down, turned round, bent down, and said right in his face, 'We ask the questions, Mr Wainwright. There are one or two things that don't add up, you see. Now tell us the truth. You were not happily married, were you? In fact your wife was frightened of you, wasn't she? Did your beatings go just a little too far and—'

'And what? You can't think that! I love my wife. I'd do anything to get her back.'

'That's not what we've heard.'

WPC Jones, who until now had not spoken but had closely regarded James Wainwright's facial expressions and noted his uncomfortable twitching, leaned towards him and said in a quiet voice, 'It's obviously a difficult time for you, but you have to realise that we must pursue every angle. It's our job.'

'But don't you see you are wasting valuable time?'

WPC Jones continued, 'You see, we look at things from all points of view, and we have heard that... well, let's just say that there were a few problems between you, weren't there?'

'What the fuck has that got to do with you? All married couples have problems. Your job is to find my wife.'

'That attitude is not helpful, sir. And I'll ask you to modify your language when you speak to a lady.'

'Helpful? Helpful? You are the ones who are supposed to be helpful. Why aren't you looking for her? And I'll bloody well use any kind of language I like in my own house. You'd better leave.'

'No need to take that attitude, sir,' said the WPC. 'Come along, Charlie, we should leave Mr Wainwright to think about things.'

'Yes, you're right,' said the PC as they walked to the door. 'Now if you feel that there is something that you want to tell us—'

Jim slammed the door. He'd heard enough. Bloody crazy! Did they really think he'd murdered his own wife? He had felt like it sometimes. Especially when she'd had that affair and had that kid. But deep down he loved her. Well, he would, if only she would love him. That's what he kept telling her. That's what made him mad enough to hit her. If only she would love him, he would trust her and he wouldn't want to hurt her. He wouldn't get mad. Just thinking about her having someone else's brat made him see red. He could feel the rage coming on now. Just wait till she got back; he'd make her bloody sorry walking out like this. He knew that she would have to come back because she thought too much about their boys to stay away for good or do anything stupid.

Although there was a blazing fire in the living room, Sarah could feel the chilly mood between the husband and wife. He was watching the TV and seemed happy to talk to her. His wife was trying to watch the children, cook the evening meal, and set the table.

'Do you think you could help instead of lying around doing nothing?' the wife said.

'I've been working all day, and I shall be putting the kids to bed when you've gone to work tonight. I need five minutes.'

'Don't we all? I wouldn't mind five minutes. What do you think I've been doing all day? Sitting on my arse? And what do you think I'll be doing at work?'

Sarah recognised the preliminaries to a full-scale domestic. This was exactly what she was trying to escape.

'I'll go back to my room now and leave you in peace,' said Sarah.

They didn't notice the irony.

Back in her ice box she shivered from cold and the memory of her own domestic hell that she had left. The scene she had just witnessed confirmed her decision. Eventually Sarah could endure the cold no longer. She threatened to leave and was given a heater. She spent the evening with her feet on top of it, reading.

The next morning she left straight after breakfast. She bought a really warm parka and caught the bus to Portree. It was another incredible journey, which wiped out the memory of the feuding family. She knew that she needed space to feel nature's energy, and she absorbed it into her body, regaining her strength. Meditating on nature cleared her mind and allowed her to see plainly what her life was like and what she needed to change. The power of the mountains filtered through her skin, and she felt it flowing into every vein and artery. She knew that she was having what was called a nervous breakdown, but the mountains were proving to be an excellent cure. In Sarah's opinion a nervous breakdown was a term used to describe someone who won't or can't conform. *I've conformed long enough*, she thought.

The route to the next island involved a coach journey and another ferry. This time it took several hours, and when she arrived in Portree it was dark. She tried several houses displaying B&B signs, but they were all full. It was bitterly cold. It got later and later. She trudged up and down what seemed to be an estate of council houses. Each enquiry led to the next street. She kept telling herself that it would be OK; there was no need to be afraid. She didn't believe herself. She started to panic. It started to rain. Finally she knocked on the door of an ordinary house. It had no signs, nothing to indicate that she would be welcome, but to her relief she was – into a warm bright cheerful family house.

Remembering last evening which she had spent miserably, she changed quickly and went out to dinner. What luxury!

After a good night's sleep and a few enquiries, she decided that the next stage of her journey would take her to Stornaway. She'd been told there was a post van, which would pick her up. She began to walk along the road to Stornaway. It was thirty miles. The information she had gleaned had led to confusion. The problem was that no one seemed to know whether the post van/bus had left or not. It was another beautiful day. It was madness to begin a thirty-mile walk, but wasn't everything she was doing mad and wouldn't it be madness to go home? She was so drunk with her own freedom and the mountain scenery that she hardly thought of the dangers. If worst came to worst, she told herself, she would knock on the door of a cottage. There would be some cottages on the roadside, surely. The fact that she hadn't seen any so far, nor had she seen any vehicles, didn't affect her optimism.

Drinking in the air like fine wine and hardly daring to believe her bounty, she strode on through the valley between the mountains which rose so high each side of her that she couldn't see the summits. As she walked she met a goat or rather a goat met her. It was a young kid who was fascinated with the toggles of her parka. He tried to eat them. No amount of petting, patting, or shooing was successful. It flatly refused to leave her side. Now she had a companion.

As she turned for the umpteenth time to see if the bus was approaching she noticed a young man walking behind her. It seemed crazy not to speak to him in this place, where there was no other sign of humanity.

'Hi, I am aiming to get to Stornaway,' she said.

'Hi, you know it's thirty miles away?'

'Yes, but they told me in the town that there was a post bus that would pick me up when it came.'

'Yes, I am hoping to get on it too. Do you know what time it was supposed to leave?'

'Nobody seemed to know. Not even whether it had left already or not. I thought I'd take a chance.'

'We can't reach Stornaway before dark if the bus doesn't come.'

'I know. I thought I would knock on a door and ask for bed and breakfast if it gets late.'

'That's a bit risky.'

'No more risky than the situation I've just left.'

'Are you on holiday?'

'Sort of. You?'

'Yes, I'm youth hostelling. What do you mean sort of?'

'I suppose you could say I am a runaway. I've left home. I am a missing person. No one knows where I am.'

'Who's no one? Your parents?'

'Well, yes, but also my husband and my children.'

'You've left your children? What made you leave your children?'

'Let's just say I'm safer here walking in the middle of nowhere and talking to total strangers than in my own home. I don't want to think about it.'

All this time the goat was nudging them and still trying to eat the toggles on their coats; it made them laugh and focus their attention on the more immediate problem.

It was all bizarre and wonderful. Sarah thought she had a guardian angel who would protect her no matter what. At least she had escaped the devil she'd been living with.

'Peep, peep.'

It was the bus.

'Thank God for that,' they both said together.

The bus stopped, and the goat leapt on board before them. Sarah and the young man couldn't stop laughing.

'You can't bring a goat on the bus,' said the driver.

'It's not ours,' they chorused.

'I'm not moving till you get it off.'

Fortunately the young man performed a feat of strength; he picked up the goat and put it off the bus.

They sat separately.

Stornaway was a town much like her home town and similar in size. It felt just right. Her lodging house was hospitable, and there was always hot water for a bath. The owner was chatty and, being recently retired and widowed, enjoyed her company. He missed his wife and his workmates.

They sat drinking tea.

'So what have you retired from?'

'I was in the police force. I was chief inspector by the time I retired,' he said.

Sarah's cup shook, and she put it back on the saucer with difficulty.

'Really,' she managed to stammer. 'That must have been an interesting job.'

Was he looking into her brain? Could he deduce that she was a missing person? He didn't act suspicious. She must be very careful.

The next day was closing day in Stornaway, so it was very quiet.

Exploring the geography of the town, she bumped into the young man – several times in fact. He said he was going to a ceildeh. He suggested that she might like to go. She said she would and arranged to meet him later.

Sarah saw no one as she walked from the B&B to the village hall. She stood looking at the moon, which hung low over the building, and wondered at the myriad stars. Millions of stars but not one person could she see. Maybe she had arrived too early or mistaken the day.

'So you didn't bring the goat then?'

Turning round she saw the young man.

'Hi! I was just...'

'I know. You were up there in another world. Wonderful, isn't it? The stars are invisible in most towns and cities because of the street lights these days, you know.'

'You are right. I can't remember the last time I gazed at the stars. It makes you feel tiny but also peaceful. You know, like the universe is so vast, our little lives are insignificant.'

'Puts everything into perspective, doesn't it?'

'I thought I'd made a mistake. Come to the wrong place. I haven't seen any people.'

Just then the door opened, and bright light illuminated a boy and a girl who came out holding hands and laughing. They walked round the side of the building into the shadows.

'There are two youngsters who are going to make the most of the moonlight.'

Sarah shuddered and remembered a time when that might have been her.

'Let's go in,' she said.

It was like entering a TARDIS. Immediately she was bathed in bright lights, loud music, and warmth. *Where on earth have all these people come from?* thought Sarah as she found a seat. They were all dancing. Everyone looked happy and carefree. She too wanted to be part of it. She wanted to be happy and carefree. The band played a jig, and she found it difficult to remain seated. Standing up she almost knocked the drinks out of the young man's hand.

'Hey, careful. I brought one for you. It's a local specialty.'

'Sorry, it's the rhythm. I can't sit still.'

'Do you know this dance?'

' "Strip the Willow," isn't it? I learnt it at school.' He put down the drinks. 'Come on then.'

Before she could think, she was weaving in and out; swinging and being swung, until she didn't know whether she was turning or the room was spinning. She couldn't stop laughing. Everybody was laughing. *This is how life should be*, she thought.

They danced nearly every dance. They didn't talk much, but she did learn that he was called Tom and that he was thirty-five. This shocked her because up until then she had thought of him as a young man; yet they were the same age. She went to the cloakroom to look in the mirror. What had happened to her? She was old before her time. She had lost her youth. Was it too late to get it back? Dancing and hearing the music had made her feel young again. It wasn't too late to live again. Maybe she could even take up the fiddle and someday play in a band like this.

On Friday morning the town was busy. Her landlord had told her about the standing stones outside the town on a hilltop. All she knew about standing stones was that they were old and mystical. She wasn't really interested in that sort of thing, but something drew her to them.

She hopped into a taxi and said, 'Can you take me to see the standing stones please?'

They arrived at the top of a hill. The driver pointed across a field and said he'd wait if she wanted to go closer. The wind was raw. It was icy cold. Touching the stones and staring out to sea she heard the wind howling and wondered, was she really here, was she dreaming, was she really free from the violence?

'You're out without that goat again,' the young man shouted above the howling wind.

'Did you follow me?' she said, feeling a little scared.

'Not at all. I walked up here from the town. I suppose that is your taxi.'

'Yes, I was just about to go back. It's so cold.'

'You don't feel the cold when you are walking uphill. I wanted to see the stones before I left.'

'You're leaving?'

'Yes. I'm not a runaway like you. I'm on holiday. I have to go back to work. Why not send the taxi away and walk back into town with me?'

So she did.

He was a man of few words, which suited her. He gently took her hand as they walked, saying, 'Do you mind?' She shook her head. It was pleasant being so close to a man and not being afraid.

When they reached the town, they parted knowing that they would never see each other again. They didn't exchange addresses or telephone numbers. He kissed her on the cheek and said, 'I hope you find what you are looking for,' and walked away.

She said nothing but wondered how long it had been since she'd felt tenderness in a kiss.

She had to make a decision. She had enough money for two weeks. She shivered at the thought of going back. She thought of the letter she had posted to her sister from Inverness. It would almost be worth going back to see peoples' faces when she told them her story. She longed to see the boys. How much did they miss her? Did they miss her more than she needed to be away from their father? She remembered the life she had left and compared it to the last two weeks. Only two weeks. And she'd suffered for fifteen years. She was scared that if she phoned them he would be in the house. They may be able to check where she was phoning from; that was, if they were looking for her. But she needed to find a way of knowing if the boys were OK. Then she had a brilliant idea. She would ring the school. They couldn't possibly expect her to ring there.

'Hello, is that St John's Comprehensive? I'm Mrs Wainwright, mother of David and Matthew.'

'Mrs Wainwright? Where are you call—'

'Is it possible to give them a message?'

'Yes, but where are you—'

'It's very important. I want them both to know that I am safe and well.'

'Mrs Wainwright, it is most—'

She put the phone down. *They will know now that I am alright. I wish I could find out about them. Please God, let them be O.K.*

Sarah went into a café and bought a cup of very strong coffee. She felt sick. Last night and this morning she had tasted a different life – life as it should be. Could she continue without news of her boys? Well, she'd survived without news of her baby, if you could call it survival. *Right. I have walked away from the violence, and now I must create a better life – a life where maybe I can send for my boys and who knows someday find my baby.*

The school secretary sat for a moment holding the receiver in mid-air.

'You'll never guess who that was,' she said, turning to the rest of the office staff. 'Mrs Wainwright. You know? The mother of David and Matthew Wainwright, the woman who went missing?'

'Is she back?'

'No, she just wanted me to tell the boys that she is OK. Can you believe that?'

'Best ring the police then. They took her husband in for questioning, you know. They think he bumped her off.'

'Really? Will this let him off the hook? Do you know him? I never liked him. He came to open day once. They say he's violent.'

'I never understand why women stay with violent men.'

'Well, it looks like this is one woman who didn't. Although it seems that she has left her children. I can't understand how a mother could ever leave her children. I think I'll tell the boys first before I tell the police.'

Sarah walked out of the café with a more determined step than when she had gone in. As she was striding confidently back to her lodgings she saw a sign in a shop window: VAN DRIVER WANTED. She had a clean driving licence. She liked driving. She went into the shop.

'I'd like to see the manager, please. I've come about the job.'

Introduction to Chapter Three

Sad to say, Sarah went back. She couldn't leave the boys. She had lost her baby; she couldn't bear to lose them too. The break renewed her strength enough to survive the marriage for a few more years before she picked up the courage to leave. James was a heavy smoker and died of lung cancer a few years later. She soon found herself caring for her mother Eva.

Sarah felt like a cardboard cut-out. She always said that that was what her mother wanted. She was afraid of the real Sarah. She wanted a Stepford daughter. Sarah had moved in to live with her mother when she was ill. When she was better Sarah moved back to her own flat. However she visited her mother three times a day; morning, afternoon and evening (to put her to bed).

Better? What is better when you are ninety-two, almost blind and deaf, and can only walk with pain and the aid of a frame? Their lives were routine, strictly routine, and controlled by time. Her mother set the alarm for six o'clock. Yes, even at ninety. Days are long when all you do is eat and pee, but nights are longer when you don't sleep and can only pee. She insisted on washing and dressing herself. It took her an hour and a half. Then she sat in her chair by the window next to the dining-room table where she spent her day.

The programme for the day read like that of a conference without substance:

Eight o'clock: breakfast

Eleven o'clock: coffee

One o'clock: lunch

Two o'clock: afternoon nap

Four o'clock: afternoon tea

Six o'clock: evening meal

Ten o'clock: Horlicks and sleeping tablet

Ten-thirty: bed

What do you do if you can't see the TV; you can't see to read; you can no longer knit or crochet because of the arthritis; you can't hear the radio; visitors are frustrating because you can't hear them, and they sit in embarrassed silence thinking, "Oh God, please don't let this happen to me"?

This is what she does: She wakens up crying although she swears that she never goes to sleep. She says there is a roomful of people all night.

'You must be dreaming,' Sarah says.

'No, no, I'm definitely not dreaming.'

'They are from the next world,' Sarah's friend says. 'They come to take her and she won't go.'

Then she sits in the bathroom crying and trying to get dressed. Sarah doesn't ask her why she is crying. Is it because she doesn't want to know? Or is it because anybody would cry in her position? Or is it because she is so used to it that she hardly notices? Perhaps if she wasn't crying, Sarah would say, 'Why aren't you crying?'

All through the day as she sits in her chair, eyes closed but not sleeping, she cries. Finally as she gets ready for bed she cries. Sarah can't stand it. She wants to shake her and yell, 'Stop bloody crying, can't you? Why are you crying? I should be crying, not you. You are here in your own house where you want to be. You are looked after. You are clean and warm and well fed. You are not in the nursing home that you dread. Yes, I know you can't see. I know you can't read. I know you can't hear. I know you can't knit. I know you can't pull your own knickers up. Why do you always focus on the negative? Just for once why can't you say, "Yes, it is a lovely morning"? But no, instead you say, "It'll be raining by dinner time".'

But Sarah doesn't shout. She doesn't say anything at all. She doesn't even grit her teeth anymore; she waits until her mother says something funny and writes it down. Not that she ever says anything intentionally funny, but like the night when she was riding upstairs on the stair lift and she said, 'The top of the grandfather clock needs dusting'.

Sarah said, 'I thought you couldn't see.'

Her mother snapped, 'I can see dust.'

Breasts

They hang

Empty

Did they feed her

All those years ago

They hang –

Limp

Yet they fed four

More years before

They hang –

Withered

They were full and round

But now

Empty, limp and withered

Like a goat-skin pouch

Parched and dry

As though the very blood has been sucked out

Children blood-suckers

Mother giver of life

Left bereft of love

(Jean Wild)

Chapter Three

Mother and Daughter

Eva sat like a frightened bird. Her life had run down and wound around her like the ball of wool which was always at her feet. It sometimes wrapped itself around her ankles when she struggled to answer the door bell. Life was enclosing her in a cocoon. She jabbed at the wraps with her knitting needles. Like the swan that swims in ever-decreasing circles on a freezing pond, she tried to keep her world open.

She was sharp. Everything about her was sharp – especially her tongue. She was so scared she picked and pecked at her daughter Sarah.

I suppose I can forgive her that. She is ninety. She is my mother, although I can't believe it. We are so different.

Nevertheless Sarah felt stabbed and wounded by her mother's words.

Eva sat for long hours alone. She talked to herself, mostly about her daughter.

Our Sarah is too sharp for her own good. Cut herself if she's not careful. Got an answer for everything she has. Nosy too, frightened of missing something. And what does she think she looks like in those earrings? Common, I call 'em. Great big dangly things. You'd never catch me wearing anything like that. That new coat she bought last week. She came in and threw it on the chair hard-faced as you like. But I told her, 'That new coat,' I said. 'Well, I don't like it. It's too gaudy for me. 'Orrible jazzy thing. What I like is a nice plain coat. All one colour. Why don't you buy yourself a nice coat?' I said.

The situation between mother and daughter was taut. It was as though an invisible wire was stretched about the house. Either of them could trip the other or themselves unexpectedly. It was as if the house was full of unexploded landmines from the last war. They both began each visit by trying to tread carefully. As is often the case in such circumstances, the result proved to be the opposite of that intended.

The old lady's mind was no more capable of avoiding a tricky situation to protect her emotions than her feet were of stepping over a trip wire to protect her body. The house became more like a battleground at each visit. After the first careful movements to avoid an explosion usually failed there often followed a rapid exchange of weapons. Remarks flashed between them like sparks. They shot and stabbed each other. The verbal weaponry came from well-stocked armouries and was delivered with deadly accuracy. On each foray, both opponents were able to penetrate the other's defenses. The daughter would retreat. The mother was unable to. She was a prisoner in her own home. Her castle had become her goal.

All Sarah ever wanted was to be recognised as the good little girl that she was and always had been. All Eva ever wanted was that her daughter would get married again and settled down.

Eva had broken her hip when she was eighty-three, and now, six years later, she could do very little. She had to prop the door open with her walking stick held in one hand while balancing her tray in the other. The tray wobbled dangerously as she slid her feet along the worn-out carpet. Almost dropping the tray on the table, she would fall into the chair in the bay window of the dining room. Life was hard.

I can't expect our Sarah to help me. I made the mistake of supporting her through college, and now she knows nothing – not even how to fold sheets. And she's gone and got herself divorced. So even if she could fold sheets, there would be no time to do it because she has to work. No time to look after her ninety-year-old mother!

One day Sarah asked her mother what it was like to be perfect. Eva fired the answer, 'I know I'm not perfect, but I do know how to fold sheets'. Sarah knew that the implication was 'any fool can fold sheets', and they both knew that she could not peg them on the washing line properly either. Eva continued, 'Waste of education, if you ask me. All those wasted years – staying on at school and then college and you can't fold sheets.'

'Why is it so important? Who says they should be folded lengthways and—'

'My mother, she took in washing, and she taught me to do it the right way.'

Eva began a demonstration, difficult though it was, with her trembling arthritic hands.

'It makes a lot of difference. When I was a child, I turned the handle on the big wooden mangle while my sister hand-fed it with sheets and tablecloths – all folded the correct way. That way they didn't need ironing.'

Sarah understood. Imagine ironing sheets with an old-fashioned flat iron! Imagine not getting paid because the sheets were crumpled!

Eva had learned her lesson well. She had been controlled all her life by a set of rules, which had become redundant. She hadn't realised it nor had been able to learn new patterns of behaviour. Sarah thought of her stainless-steel automatic washing machine and tumble dryer and wondered when she had last ironed a garment.

Sheet folding was not Sarah's only weakness. There were lots of things that she could not do after she had walked out through her mother's front door. It was like entering a TARDIS. Outside she was strong, confident, outgoing, and happy. As she closed the front door and passed the grandfather clock in the hallway she changed into a total incompetent. The only comforting fact was that she was not the only one to be affected this way. The same fate had been suffered by six-foot he-men.

Gerald, Eva's son-in-law, was usually capable, confident, and efficient. All those things. He even thought he could make a cup of tea. Sarah overheard her mother's sucking through the teeth sound 'ffffffffffff', which could pierce one's very soul, followed by, 'He's done it again'.

Anyone listening would have thought that he'd at least put arsenic in her tea.

'What have I done?' asked Gerald.

'You've wet the sugar spoon.'

Sarah smiled, partly because she thought it was funny but mostly because for once she wasn't on the sharp end.

The Neighbours

What the neighbours would think was the controlling message engraved long ago on the internal tape recorder in Eva's head. She no longer knew, if in fact she ever had, what she thought, but she knew damned well what the neighbours thought. She might often forget their names. But, my God, she never forgot what they thought!

Sarah, however, had views of her own. She tried to avoid the neighbours. But she also knew what the neighbours would think because her mother frequently began a sentence with, "The neighbours will think..."

Mind you, it wasn't exactly what the neighbours thought that was the problem. It was more the way that Eva said, 'What will the neighbours think?' that implied that they could have such unbelievably disapproving thoughts. It was a problem not for Sarah but for Eva because she must have had the thoughts in the first place in order to say, 'What would the neighbours think?' in such a way as to imply that their thoughts would be disapproving.

The Iron Hand in the Iron Glove

Eva ruled her house like a sergeant major. Everything obeyed her. The cutlery lay to attention in the drawers as did her underwear. The sheets and pillow cases on the beds did not dare to wrinkle or crease. Her offspring in earlier years had slept to attention for the same reason.

Eva's regime was strict, and it never varied. Everyday was reserved for a different task, and each task had a set routine. She had rules too. 'There's a place for everything, and I like everything in its place', she was often heard to say. This had practical advantages. Everyone knew exactly where everything was. In fact if a teaspoon got accidentally left on the draining board – and God forbid that this should happen but if it did—it would certainly not be due to Eva's carelessness. If a teaspoon did get left, it would be so conditioned and scared that it would leap back to the left-hand kitchen drawer to join the rest of the cutlery which would be lying to attention.

The garden too came under Eva's command. The weeds did not dare to grow. Plants, which vaguely resembled weeds, had very short lives.

The grass never needed cutting as it did not dare to grow higher than the regulation half inch. It was the same with the privet hedge. In 1974, the hedge grew too high and was dug out by its roots. That seemed to be lesson enough for the rest.

She disliked autumn. All those blasted leaves blowing all over the place! Eva thought them untidy and downright unsightly. Sarah noted that for all that they rarely landed in her mother's garden. She thought they must have had an arrangement with the wind to transport them elsewhere.

Uncharacteristically Eva fed the birds. However, there were never any crumbs to be seen. Sarah thought that she had trained the birds to swoop and catch the crumbs in mid-flight so that they wouldn't land in the garden.

Eva enjoyed the control of her domain, and she knew exactly where its boundaries lay. The curtains had to be drawn at the first signs of darkness, and she was fanatical about not allowing even the tiniest chink of light to escape. If a tiny pinhole of light dared to appear, the curtain was firmly secured with a drawing pin. In this Sarah's father, Arthur, colluded. The house was a bastion against the outside world. Arthur was Eva's ally, and each evening they defended themselves against the enemy. Both of them having lived through two world wars, they had internalised the need for an enemy. None being apparent, they created imaginary ones.

Arthur had fitted locks on the windows. The front and back doors were triple locked, and even the internal doors had alarms.

Sarah was mildly amused by this security. She believed that had the enemy penetrated this fortress in an attempt to steal any of the contents, it would have been a waste of time. Why? Because the contents of the house were so afraid of the regime that they would not have allowed themselves to be stolen. In the unlikely event of a successful robbery, the goods stolen would surely have quickly returned themselves to their rightful places before their loss was discovered by the iron hand.

Outside of this regime Eva recognised that she had absolutely no control whatsoever. She ruled, and ruled well, in her domain. Elsewhere she expected others to be responsible and to rule with the same fanaticism – not that she called it 'fanaticism', but she called it 'doing the right thing'.

Anyone who did not do as she did was obviously doing the wrong thing and was stupid or lazy or both.

Sarah remained an enigma to Eva. In Eva's eyes, she rarely did the right thing. What's more, she argued about what was right and wrong bringing information into the conversation, which made Eva feel uncomfortable.

Sarah was a vegetarian. Eva knew that eating meat was 'the right thing' because she'd always eaten meat. It was good for you. Eva assumed that Sarah was a vegetarian because she wanted to lose weight. Eva could think of no other reason for not eating every scrap of food on your plate. When you've been poor and hungry and lived through rationing, leaving food was not an option.

One meal time Sarah said, 'There are lots of reasons why I do not eat meat, but losing weight is not one of them.'

Eva replied, 'Go on, have a slice of lamb. It's tender and really juicy. You'll enjoy it.'

Sarah responded, 'I hope the lamb is enjoying it too.'

Eva squirmed but said, 'Well, what would we do with them if we didn't eat them? We'd be overrun with them.'

Sarah thought, *There's no answer to that*, and imagined a world overrun with gambolling lambs.

Feet and Footwear

Eva never went out of the house. She did go out of the room where her chair was. She went into the kitchen, and she had a stair lift to take her upstairs. For this she needed footwear. But not any kind of footwear would do for Eva's feet.

Eva had been one of eight children and had been so poor that she had squashed her feet into any and every size and shape of boot or shoe that happened to come her way. This was out of necessity since, being one of ten living in a back-to-back house, there was little room indoors and she had to spend as much time as possible outside.

Outside was an unmade, rough, stony, and puddle-filled road next to a canal. So at ninety, Eva's feet told the story of her cruel childhood. They were terribly and horribly deformed. The second toe on each foot was pushed completely out of place and was bent at right angles. She had corns and bunions and calluses. So Sarah found it impossible to find footwear for her mother, which she could actually wear, not to mention comfort.

Sarah had bought every kind of footwear imaginable, and Eva had tried it and declared it uncomfortable. The largest-fitting, double EE lace-ups, wide-fitting open-toed sandals, zip-up suede boots, canvas beach shoes, even espadrilles – all had been tried and had failed. Sarah became weary and had long since stopped seeing the funny side. Each pair of shoes was too small, too narrow, too high, too low, or too anything but right. She returned them for larger, wider, higher, and lower only to find that they were still uncomfortable. Eva said often to Sarah, 'Return them and get your money back.' That was easier said than done. Sarah felt defeated.

Sometimes she tried to wear the shoes herself; often they remained on the back seat of her car. It was not unusual to see three full shoe boxes sitting there. Some would be on the way to be tried on. Some had been tried and were on their way back to the shop. Others were just left there because Sarah was too embarrassed to return them to the shop for a third time.

Over the years they had discovered that sheepskin slippers were satisfactory. Luckily Sarah was not vegan. Discovering that sheepskin slippers were satisfactory did not, however, solve the problem entirely. Eva could no longer raise her feet, so she had to slide them along the floor. Sliding needs a slippery surface, so slippers without added rubber soles had to be found, which was not easy. Secondly, because they were subjected to constant friction, they quickly produced holes. Thirdly, they had to have a lace which could be tied in a bow on top to enable loosening and tightening to accommodate the swelling of Eva's feet.

Now, buying sheepskin slippers in winter poses few problems. Summer is a different kettle of fish. I have only seen sheepskin slippers on sale in Wales in the summer. Everyone who ever visited Eva and a few people who hadn't somehow found themselves enlisted in the sheepskin-slipper hunt. The home help, the neighbours, the meals on wheels lady, the district nurse, Sarah's boss, Sarah's friends – anyone who went to Wales for a week, weekend, or even a day – dutifully came back with a pair of sheepskin slippers. Frequently Sarah saw them coming up the path with a shoe box under their arm, then almost as frequently returning to their cars with the box still in place, muttering, 'She said sheepskin. Ungrateful old devil!' Sarah smiled and wondered, what was it this time? Rubber sole? No lace? Wrong size? At least she wouldn't have to wear them.

Library Books

Eva read, did her knitting, and listened to the radio – all in the same room from the same chair. She ate her meals in the same chair by the table next to the window. She had the telephone on the table so that she could use it without moving. She ate sweets from a cupboard nearby, which she could reach from her chair. But she could not change her library books. Sarah changed her library books. She did this when the pile on the right reached four. There were two piles on the sideboard, within reach of the chair, of course. The ones on the right were unread, and the pile on the left had been read and needed changing. Sarah breathed a sigh of relief when she placed five or six books on the right-hand pile thinking that would do for another week. But remember, Sarah was stupid and couldn't even fold sheets, so what chance did she have choosing library books?

'You know I like a good story,' Eva would say. 'I've told you often enough.'

Sarah was foolish enough to bring books that she had read and enjoyed herself. Eva would greet her with, 'I don't know what you've brought me this week. I'm not reading that rubbish. Why don't you ask the librarian to choose me some nice stories?'

Sometimes Sarah chose books at random, and if they were written by women and had a 'nice' picture on the front, she thought they would be all right. The result was that the left-hand pile would be four high the next day, and she would be greeted with, 'They've got that word in! I've told you not to bring me books with that word in. I'll not read another page. Disgusting! There's no need for it.'

Sarah was at a loss as to what to do. Sometimes she tried to scan the books for 'that word', but she only had an hour for dinner and she did like to eat. Once when she was doing this, she noticed an old gentleman watching her.

Feeling embarrassed, she blurted out, 'I'm just looking for four-letter words for my mother—'

And before she could explain he'd walked away, muttering, 'You'd think her mother would have more taste.'

So she'd gone to the librarian and asked, 'Do any of these books have four-letter words in them?'

The librarian had answered, 'No, these are the ones you want over here.'

'No, no, you don't understand. They are not for me. They are for my mother.'

Sarah heard the old gentleman behind her again, 'Her mother! Disgusting! What's the world coming to?'

There was no time to explain as her dinner hour was over, and she dared not be late for her first class of the afternoon. Fortunately as Eva's memory was poor, if she made no complaint about the books, Sarah wrote a tiny letter 'A' in the back in pencil and after a couple of weeks they were found on her mother's sideboard for a second or even a third time.

The Home Help

Eva relied mainly on Jennifer, the home help, to do her housework. Jennifer arrived weekday mornings supposedly to help her to get dressed and to get her breakfast. Eva, however, was fiercely independent and was always dressed, washed, and breakfasted by the time Jennifer arrived.

This was no mean feat. It took a phenomenal amount of strength, courage, and determination. She set the alarm for six and rose immediately she heard it ring. It then took her an hour to dress and wash and a further one hour to make and eat a bowl of porridge and drink a pot of tea. By the time Jennifer arrived at eight thirty only the housework remained.

This was part of Eva's plan. She was fanatical about housework. Since she could no longer kneel down to clean floors, nor manipulate the Hoover, nor even use a duster, she made sure that she was ready to supervise Jennifer. She wanted the job done properly her way, the right way, and she used all her energy to ensure that standards in her house did not fall.

Jennifer did not understand Eva's methods, and she was doomed to failure. She could never reach perfection because that would have left Eva redundant. Also, how could she admit that it was possible to reach her standards in a couple of years? Eva had spent her life cleaning professionally from the age of twelve. She was proud to know that she could clean better than anyone and had always done a good job. How could Jennifer understand that Eva enjoyed it when she was less than perfect, because Eva could show her superiority and skills? So the harder Jennifer tried, the more faults Eva found. And the worse Jennifer felt, the better Eva felt.

Eva complained bitterly to Sarah about the home help; she did not refer to her by name but called her 'she'.

'She doesn't clean upstairs properly, you know. She was only up there for twenty minutes. You can't clean upstairs properly in twenty minutes.

'She is very wasteful, you know. She wastes the bleach, the washing-up liquid, and the disinfectant. She used a whole bottle of disinfectant this morning. I bet she doesn't waste stuff at home like that. It's criminal.

'She's clumsy too. She's always knocking things over and breaking them. And she pulls the plugs out by the wires.

'She's lazy, y' know. Just look at this carpet. I could do better myself if I could push the vacuum cleaner.'

When the home help was ill and could not come at all for about two weeks, another woman took her place. Sarah suggested that Eva might like to phone Jennifer. So she did.

'Hello, Jennifer. How are you? Now, don't you come back to work till you are really better. You look after yourself.

'How am I?

'Oh I'm not too bad... well (*sob*), I'm not feeling too good (*sob, sob*). In fact I'm feeling a bit depressed (*sob, sob, sob*). Well, I miss you. Oh yes, Margaret comes, but she doesn't do it like you. I miss you. I'll be much better when you come back to work.

'Bye for now. Get better soon.'

Sarah smiled to herself but said to her mother, 'I thought you didn't like her?'

'I never said that. She's like a daughter to me.'

The Ritual

Eva did the same things at the same time every day. Not keeping to her timetabled routine upset her. The reverse was true for Sarah. At night the pattern went like this:

'Good night. God bless,' said Eva.

'Good night,' said Sarah, stepping onto the landing and pulling the bedroom door to but not closing it.

'Don't close the door. Just pull it to.'

Sarah felt this repetition excruciating. She gritted her teeth to prevent obscenities from escaping. She tensed her body to ensure that the rage was internalised and not transferred into a dance of anger. She let her mind wander and wondered what it would be like if one night she did flip.

Stepping onto the landing she would stand feet astride, arms outstretched, and scream – scream at the top of her voice. Then she would pick up Eva's walking stick and beat out a rhythm on the bedroom doors. She would grab a toilet roll—no, two—no, three (there was always a good stock just there on the drawers; Sarah always made sure that there was, on Eva's instructions)—unfurl them, and hurl them like party streamers down the stairs. Then she would stand on the stair lift and set it in motion. She would shout and stamp on the ride down, banging the walls and ceiling with the walking stick as she went. When she reached the hall, she would leap off; she would use the bed warmer as a gong and the radiator as a wash board and then...

'You've forgotten the landing light,' Eva called.

Eva's words penetrated Sarah's internal rampage and put a stop to such nonsense.

Sarah locked up safely: back-door chain, key and bolt, kitchen-door chain, lounge-door chain, dining-room key, front-door chain, bolt and triple lock.

And she thought, *How many more times will I have to lock up safely?*

Cemeteries and Crematoriums

'Is it snowing?' Sarah asked as she brushed what she thought were snowflakes from her shoulders. She looked up at the sky. There *were* particles of something floating down.

'It's cold enough,' someone said.

Funny colour for snow, thought Sarah. *It's more like— Oh my God, it's ashes! It's my Auntie Nancy's ashes!*

She looked up again, and this time she spotted the chimney. Sure enough the smoke coming from the crematorium's chimney was being blown their way as they descended the steps to return to the funeral cars.

Two days later they were back again. This time it was her father's ashes, which landed on and around them as they returned to the funeral cars.

Sarah was getting used to funerals, but she had never had to arrange one herself before. A year earlier it had been her sister and in between a friend's son, aged fourteen and two work colleagues and a neighbour. So now Eva and Sarah had relied on the funeral director for advice, and everything had gone smoothly. But a few days after the funeral they discovered that Arthur's ashes had been buried under a square foot of grass in what looked like the middle of a football field. They were both stunned. Eva had been used to burials not cremations and had dutifully put flowers on her parents' graves every Xmas until she became confined to the house.

'What do you do when there is no grave?' she asked Sarah.

Sarah felt guilty because she didn't know. She remembered reading some information about plaques and memorial walls and seats. But she had thought that her father's name would automatically appear on the memorial scroll and that they could decide about the rest later. A map arrived in the post; it looked like graph paper with a cross on it. It took some time to work out what it meant. It was a bit like those games you play at autumn fairs: pay 10p and place your cross to find the buried treasure. Eva couldn't understand it at all. So Sarah said she would take her and show her where it was.

It was a wet day when they went on this bizarre treasure hunt. Eva, at ninety, was barely able to walk. She was, of course, wearing her sheepskin slippers, which, incidentally, had developed holes in the soles and proved no match for the elements. So the two of them shuffled along at a snail's pace in the searing wind, which, by this time, had reached gale force. The rain beat down on their uncovered heads, and they huddled closer together; but there was no warmth in this closeness. Eva was stiff like a stick. Sarah summoned all her strength and stiffened her body to support her mother's weight. It took an unimaginable effort of will to restrain her steps to keep in time with Eva's. Sarah wanted to break into a run, which would take her to that spot marked 'x' and back to the car in minutes. She would also be warmed by the process. Instead here she was in slow motion, each slithered step shorter than the last. Sarah fleetingly experienced a nightmare in which they would never reach that bloody spot but would both die on the way.

Finally they reached an access point. Sarah left her mother swaying perilously in the wind. She could go no further without walking on the grass, which was sodden with the rain and certainly not to be walked upon in sheepskin slippers with holes. Sarah found the spot and pointed.

'This is it,' she screamed, her voice competing with the howling gale.

A few autumn leaves, which by some miracle had remained on this windswept hillside, swirled between them.

Sarah thought she heard her mother reply, 'Let's get back in the car.'

She rushed back to the swaying stick which surely would have snapped if Sarah hadn't caught her elbow. The journey back to the car was even worse. It was uphill. Eva's slippers left her feet, and Sarah had to retrieve them, leaving the swaying stick over and over each time she did so.

The visit left them unhappier than ever. Sarah was surprised not to have been given her father's ashes in an urn after the funeral. Eva was now visualising herself buried on this bleak anonymous hillside.

Sarah thought about this too, and about her father and mother – two souls tormented for all eternity. Something had to be done. Sarah told Eva that they could get permission to have her father's remains exhumed. Eva decided that he could then be placed in his own mother's grave, and when her time came, her ashes could be buried in her mother's grave.

Sarah undertook the task of letter writing and making phone calls, but her enthusiasm soon waned. She managed to get permission to exhume Arthur's ashes but then she had to obtain permission to rebury them in the cemetery. There were many cemeteries in the city, and one man was in charge of them all. He spent time at each cemetery. He was never at the one she rang.

At this point Eva began to have doubts. How would they know they had the right ashes? How big a container would they need? How much space would they take up? How far down did they need to dig?

Sarah began to have dreams of great big solid coffins with real dead bodies in them and enormous headstones. Then one day when Sarah was giving her mother the latest progress report, right out of the blue Eva said, 'He was a rotten old sod. He can stay where he is.'

A year later Sarah asked Eva if she would like to go to the crematorium as it was the first anniversary; they now had a wheelchair and it would not be quite so traumatic. The problem raised its head again. They still had done nothing further.

So Sarah said, 'We could plant a tree. Some people plant trees.'

'Where would we plant it?' asked Eva.

'What about bulbs?' suggested Sarah.

'If we don't know where to plant a tree, how would we know where to plant bulbs? You can't beat a good old-fashioned headstone.'

'Yes, but they are not allowed in the crematorium.'

'Well, I'm not spending all that money on a memorial seat; I would never be able to sit on it anyway.'

'We could get his name put on that scroll. Then it would be displayed on his anniversary.'

'I bet them next door didn't have a name on a scroll.'

The Doctor

Eva placed the status of the doctor in the realms of the gods. He could do no wrong. He could cure anything and everything. He was never to be kept waiting. He was always to be believed. His instructions were to be followed to the last. Sarah expected her mother to either curtsey or kneel down before him when they visited the surgery. When the doctor visited Eva at home – and these occasions were rare, very rare, even at ninety – Sarah thought it seemed wrong for Eva to be in bed and the doctor standing at her bedside. It should have been the doctor in bed and her mother administering help.

Eva made sure that he was never kept waiting at the door, not even for a second. There had to be a chair placed ready for him to sit on and a table for him to write the prescription – the prescription which was akin to magic. It had to be fetched straightaway, and Eva knew it would work, and work, immediately. If it wasn't immediately effective, then it must be her own fault, not the doctor's. Perhaps she had taken too little or too much or she had taken it too early or too late.

Who would dare argue that this was not in fact true? Certainly not Sarah. After all Eva was ninety and in reasonably good health. Any problems that occurred now were down to age. And that, she frequently said, was her fault for living too long, not the doctor's.

When Eva was eighty-eight, Sarah, on the request of the doctor, had taken her to the hospital to see a consultant. You can imagine the deference that Eva afforded the 'specialist' as she called him.

Whilst they waited – and they waited a long time – Sarah wondered how her mother would cope with being in a wheelchair in the consultant's presence. She was afraid that she might insist on crawling in and kissing his feet.

They waited and waited, not daring to go to the toilet or to get a drink. As Eva said, 'We may be called anytime, and we must not keep him waiting.'

Sarah, however, thought she would complain. It was a disgrace keeping a woman of her mother's age waiting all this time. But she knew that her mother would not allow her to leave her side in case they were called.

Finally when they were 'called', the consultant turned out to be an overgrown schoolboy. Sarah wondered why he wasn't in school uniform. This was really ridiculous. He asked Eva a couple of questions, wrote something on a card, and said, 'Well, Mrs Goodwin, you won't have to come again.'

Sarah opened her mouth to speak about her thoughts and feelings, which had been multiplying whilst they had waited, but Eva raised her hand and said in that voice that defies argument, 'Come along. We mustn't waste the doctor's time.'

The End

Sarah had heard her mother often say, 'I'm ready any time. I've had my life, and I don't want to be a trouble to others.' This was after her ninetieth birthday, which had been a milestone in many ways. She had struggled for the few years leading up to it. Life had become increasingly more difficult. Sarah's father had been very needy, and they had argued more and more over smaller and smaller things. Now she had reached two milestones together: widowhood and ninety. Eva's husband had died a few days before that birthday.

Sarah had noted frequently during that last decade that her parents lived to spite each other. They were both aware that they were trying to outlive each other. It was never voiced, of course, but it was very loud in their heads.

After these two milestones Sarah waited. She organised more and more help as her mother became frailer. She listened to her mother complaining that she was living too long. Sarah expected each visit to be her last.

Sometimes Sarah took her mother out in the newly acquired wheelchair. She noticed that friends and neighbours called more frequently. She bought some vitamin c tablets hoping to cheer her, to which she commented, 'I want something to help me to die, not to keep me alive.'

One day Sarah arrived to find a neighbour sitting with her mother who was in tears.

'We are waiting for the doctor,' the neighbour explained.

This is it, thought Sarah.

'Are you in pain, Mother?'

'I felt ill. So I rang for the doctor, and I asked Margaret to come and wait with me. Now I feel better, and I don't want the doctor to think I'm wasting his time.'

The doctor came and went.

Eva gave Sarah quite clear instructions about her funeral.

'I don't know what all the fuss is about,' said Eva. We all end up in the earth whatever happens. It's all the same. Burn me and scatter the ashes. What difference does it make where you put them?'

However, Eva did care what she looked like in her coffin. She had chosen the dress that she wanted to be laid out in. It was hanging to attention on the right-hand side of the wardrobe in the front bedroom, awaiting its hour of glory, not daring to move or get creased.

The vitamin tablets disappeared, so Sarah bought some more. The weeks turned into months and the months to years. Each birthday went by and was celebrated with a cake. It became clear to Sarah that another milestone had appeared on the horizon.

Who could blame Eva for seeing one hundred illuminated in neon lights and who could blame her for wanting to reach it?

Only when we acknowledge genuine feelings are we free from depression.

[Dorothy Rowe]

Chapter Four
Ward 101

During the period of caring for her mother, Sarah's life had become colourless. It wasn't black and white either. That would have been more interesting. It was grey, one tone of grey. Shades of grey would have been variety. It was flat, two dimensional.

Sarah drove to a lonely spot in the middle of Delemere Forest and attached a pipe from the exhaust to the inside of the car. She took a handful of sleeping tablets and lay down expecting to go into a deep sleep from which she would never awake. As she lay wondering why so many tablets had not induced sleep, she became scared – not scared of dying but of living. Somewhere she had learned that carbon monoxide poisoning, if not lethal, could certainly damage the brain. She became more and more worried that she was not going to die but that she would live in a vegetative state. Fearing that and thinking that it would be infinitely worse, she roused herself, took off the pipe, got in the driver's seat, and drove home. Well, she drove to her mother's house where she had been living while nursing her mother and went to bed.

Unbelievably she heard her mother's alarm, which even at the age of ninety Eva never forgot to set for six o'clock. She rose, went as usual to dress her, and then went downstairs to get Eva's breakfast. Fortunately or unfortunately, whichever way you look at it, Sarah's mother was almost blind. So she didn't notice that Sarah was having trouble staying awake; the sleeping tablets had well and truly kicked in by now. She didn't hear too well either, so she didn't notice Sarah's slurred speech. As soon as she could Sarah cleared away the breakfast things and crawled back upstairs. *She won't need me till eleven when she has her coffee*, she thought as she dropped onto the bed.

But the phone by her bed kept ringing. Each time she answered it she told her friends that she had taken a couple of sleeping tablets and was having a lie-in and didn't want to be disturbed, but the doorbell rang. She heard voices and footsteps on the stairs, and when she opened her eyes, she saw that her bed was surrounded by people. One of them sat on the bed, took her hand, and leaned over to talk to her.

'How many tablets did you take? When did you take them?'

The voice was unfamiliar; it said, turning to the others, 'She'll have to go to hospital.'

Sarah just wanted to sleep. Even when she arrived at the hospital, they wouldn't let her sleep. They kept making her walk to different offices, dayrooms, and wards and asked the same questions over and over.

Eventually the tablets wore off, and Sarah found herself in ward 101, the ward which she and all her friends knew to be the ward for people with mental illness. They also knew that mental illness was diagnosed when women, and sometimes men, could not or chose not to conform to the social mores.

(Sarah's best friend Kate had died at forty-two. First she had had breast cancer, then secondaries in her womb. While she was waiting for a hysterectomy, they found a brain tumour which was too large for surgery. They had been treating her for migraine for two years. Sarah had often discussed insanity and 'madness making' situations with her. Kate had received lots of therapy and had written down some of her experiences, which she managed to turn into very funny but also painful reading.)

As she came out of her semi-drugged state she noticed that the date was 5 May, the anniversary of her friend Kate's death. She wished that Kate was here to share this experience with her. *She is the only one who could understand my situation*, she thought. She longed for that deep empathy that they had shared. *I know. I'll write her a letter.*

Letter to My Dead Friend

Ward 101

City General Hospital

Dear Kate,

As you can see by my address they got me at last. I think it was the pink flowered leggings that gave me away. Remember the Fold's and Bentley Test, 'Have you found yourself wearing bright clothes lately?'

When William came to visit in a purple and yellow shirt – the jazziest I've ever seen and which he bought from an Oxfam shop – I told him he'd better watch out or he wouldn't be going home.

Well, here we are. Ten women, ten beds.

There's Sheila in the corner. She rarely makes an appearance except at mealtimes, which she never misses. I don't think I have ever seen such an expressionless face or heard such an expressionless voice. I have tried to talk to her. It went something like this:

'How are you feeling today, Sheila?'

'All right. Thank you.'

'Hi, Sheila. Would you like a cup of tea?'

'No, thank you.'

'Would you like more bread, Sheila?'

'Yes, please.'

All in the same monotonous deadpan voice.

Occasionally she has outbursts. She objects very loudly to the vulture in the next bed. I wonder if it is the one from *Jungle Book* with the voice of Ringo Starr or just a common or garden vulture. Either way it is perched there waiting to snatch up Sheila's carefully guarded stores of stolen food, which she eats behind closed curtains. She frequently threatens to inform 'The Sentinel' and to sue the staff and then... well, it's a bit unclear what would happen next.

Once I evoked a whole sentence from her. She told me that she attended a day centre. I asked her which group she was in.

'Communications,' she replied, without a flicker.

Then there is Joan. I first saw Joan crawling past my bed on her hands and knees. I called the nurse who said, 'Now, Joan, what are you doing?'

'I am crawling on my hands and knees.'

(Ask a stupid question...)

I discovered later that Joan's feet were crushed. She had jumped from the top of a multi-storey car park and had landed on her feet. The surgeons 'saved' them by putting them back together like a jigsaw puzzle. Now the arthritic pain is excruciating. She had jumped because she heard a voice which told her to jump. She hears lots of voices, and they have names. Another of the voices is called Fluffy Bum. Fluffy Bum wanted her to buy condoms, she told me.

'What for?' I asked.

'To wear,' she replied.

Always the logician.

Seneta.

Seneta is a big, beautiful, black West Indian woman. She walks with that wonderful West Indian saunter and has a superb sculptured head; around it she wraps a scarf which enhances her beauty. She conducts a church service in which she plays all the members of the congregation.

She's the little girl giggling.

She's the angry mother: 'Look at her wicked chil'.'

She's the minister: 'Pray, child, pray,'

If you didn't see her, you would think there was a whole roomful of people.

After the 'Service' she goes around the ward beseeching us all to be baptised: 'You have to receive the body and soul of Christ. The soul is going to heaven, to Jesus. The body becomes dust. There is no doubt. You must get baptised.'

She houses another woman in her head called Mary Fryer. She tries to rid herself of this lodger, but she will not move.

'I really hate you, Mary Fryer. Go away. Leave me alone. Fuck off, you filthy prostitute. Go away, you dirty nigger.'

There is a beguiling child in there too, who approaches other patients: 'Excuse me. Please can I have a cigarette? Do you mind?' she begs in a whiny overly polite voice.

'Oh thank you, thank you so much.'

Rona is an Asian woman from a Muslim family. She dresses in colourful shimmering saris and wears regulation uncut shiny black hair down to her waist. It is always immaculately brushed. Her smile is as shiny as her hair, and she wears it twenty-four hours a day. She asks everyone how they are. She clears the tables after every meal. She washes the dishes more than anyone else.

She can tell you stories to make your hair curl. She tells horror stories of blood and knives and hatchets and broken bones and fractured skulls; stories of police and court; prison stories of fear and terror and nightmares of shame; of the guilt of slashed wrists and of overdoses. Her mouth never loses the smile while she relates these stories. Her eyes never smile, for these are not fictional stories; they are the realities of her life. I listen dumbstruck as she tells me how her drunken husband gambled away her dowry and then their house.

And yet there are still more, but they are the ones that she only hints at – the ones that happened even before her marriage – a marriage which was supposed to take her away from the horror. They are the ones she may never tell. She may never tell them because she has had more than twenty treatments of ECT. I thought I was in *The Women's Room* by Marilyn French when Rona described exactly what happened in that treatment room. I know that one of the after effects of ECT is memory loss. Perhaps it is better that she has forgotten them. The saddest part is that I think she remembers the facts, but she has anaesthetized herself against the feelings. But maybe that is a good thing.

Her fixed smile is becoming slightly more crooked each day. She moves her mouth into a remembered shape and accompanies it with a noise which kind of resembles a laugh. But she has long since forgotten the appropriate times for this response. The sad part is that she probably will never remember what feelings should promote these bodily functions. That's Rona.

Barbara told me that she hears voices telling her to be a white witch. I thought of you, Kate. Maybe it is you, you old buggar.

'What do they tell you to do?' I ask.

'She is a white witch, and she tells me to do benevolent things.'

'Like what?' I ask.

'She wants me to poison my husband.'

OK, OK, Kate. I know you, and I probably think that would be benevolent. But the *normal* majority would not do it. See now, the problem in here is trying to learn what is acceptable as normal.

Anyway, back to Barbara's white witch. She also wants her to go to college. She tells her long words the meanings of which she doesn't know. I was going to ask her more about this, but she went home quite suddenly. I think she got frightened when I supported her and the white witch. I told her where she could go to find out about going to college. However, she was afraid of upsetting her husband who apparently needed her presence all day! Then she said that he had decided to go to college to take a photography course. Yes, yes, Kate, I know it is a classic case, but it's only you and I who think so. And in fact now it is only I, since you can no longer support me in this mad, mad world. Barbara and her husband are Jehovah's Witnesses!!!

A group of us went home for the weekend. When we came back on Sunday evening, I thought I had walked into a roomful of Stepford wives.

'I went to Sainsbury's on Saturday morning,' said one woman.

'I managed to do the washing and ironing,' said another.

'I left my husband some frozen meals to last him the week,' said a third.

'We had eight people for lunch today,' said a fourth.

'Oh my God! Who cooked and washed up?' I asked.

'I did,' she said. Her name is Gwen. Gwen is sixty-two but looks younger and appears well – that is until you get close, and you realise that she is near to tears all the time. I have never seen her cry. I wonder if she ever does. She has spent her life caring for others.

'What did you do?' they asked me.

How could I tell them what I had done? They would think I was mad. I went to the theatre on Friday evening. I played fiddle for the Morris Team on Saturday in a folk festival. I went to music workshops on Sunday and played fiddle all day.

So I replied, 'Oh, it was alright. I went out a bit and stayed in a bit.'

I felt ashamed. I had not done the washing and wondered if they could smell the knickers and socks I was wearing for the third day running.

So the Stepford wives have spent their lives caring and catering for other people. When the caring stops, they have no reason to get up in the morning. They can't function. They cannot care for themselves. They no longer know what they think or feel except in relation to other people's needs. They have given themselves away, and now there is nothing left. Even when they are offered something, they are unable to receive it. How many times are we told that it is better to give than to receive? These women certainly learned that lesson well. They have passed that test with honours. Unfortunately they can't do anything else, and now there is no one left for them to give to.

I listen to the Stepford wives and feel guilty. They are desperate to care for someone, but what they really need is to be cared for. *I* have a very good life, thank you very much, but I am wracked with guilt because I am not giving away my whole self to serve others. My emotional antennae are out, and I recognise great needs. I also recognise my own. I try to meet both, but in doing so I induce mountains of guilt. Do I have to give up my life to serve others and therefore die? I cannot commit suicide. I would rather do that than become a Stepford wife. So, do I live and therefore suffer the guilt? Catch-22.

Is that why you died, Kate? You said at the end that you couldn't live for anyone else and that you couldn't live for yourself.

Missing you more than ever,

Sarah

Same Hospital Two Days Later

Dear Kate,

I have to tell you more about this place. It is so bad I hardly know where to begin.

I forgot to tell you about Cheryl. She told me that she was suffering from post-natal depression. That's what the doctors had diagnosed. This was her second time in ward 101 following a birth. However, from the story that she told me of her own childhood, I learnt that like most depressives she had a well of repressed anger. She had been abused as a child as had most of the women in here. Those who were not abused in childhood were abused as adults by their husbands. For Cheryl, the only way she could release her pain was to self harm. The job of the professionals, it seems, is to prevent her from self-harm and not to find out why she is hell bent on suicide. The result is that a pattern has been set up. Cheryl spends her time working out how to trick the staff, and they spend their time watching her and trying to scupper her plans. The truth is that she doesn't really want to die. I doubt if she knows what she wants, but when she beats the staff and they find her half dead and then save her life, they both think they are winners.

Her wrists are covered in scars from the wrist-slashing attempts, and I last saw her when she was under thirty six-hour surveillance. She had somehow unlocked the bathroom window during the day and then in the night had climbed through it. Apparently it had taken five burly men to hold her down while they sedated her. Of course she wanted to be caught. Where would she run to except home to her children whom she *didn't* want to leave? But at the same time she could not cope with caring for them as she was the one who needed the care and the only way she knew how to get it was by playing the 'I'm going to kill myself' game. Catch-22 again.

I haven't mentioned the men. You won't believe this, Kate, but we are in a mixed ward! Yes. Women who have all been abused in some way by men and who by their behaviour are showing that they are trying to escape men are put in a hospital ward *with* them. The men have beds altogether at one end, and the women have the other half. All the beds have curtains around them. That makes me feel really safe!!!

The men have to walk past the women's beds to get to the day room and the dining area. I find this incredible. If the staff do not understand this simple basic need for women to feel safe, then what hope is there?

I have noticed that the main difference between the men and the women is that the depressed women self-harm, and the depressed men hit out and harm others.

Love,

Sarah

After she left hospital Sarah thought that she would like the staff to understand a little of what it feels like to be a patient in ward 101, so she wrote the following letter.

> 10 High Street
>
> Anytown
>
> England

Dear Staff of Ward 101,

I would like you all to sleep in ward 101. Just one night would be enough. The beds are really comfortable and warm, and you would be able to draw the pretty flowered curtains around your bed and make your own private little sanctum. Then you could get into bed, switch off your own little bedside light, curl up, and snuggle down for the night.

Would you like that?

I would wait until you had gone into a deep sleep. Oh, by the way, the central lights will be left on, just so that I can see you should you get up in the night. This is for your benefit, of course. Yes, I know it is difficult to sleep with florescent lights, but we do need to observe your movements for your safety.

Have you ever found sounds disturbing? I'm not talking about noises in the head. I mean noises outside your head. Loud noises which make your whole body vibrate – like the front door of ward 101 when it BANGS. Perhaps after your night in ward 101 you will bring in a decibel counter. It really is over the limit. More of that later.

OK, so there you are all tucked up in your cosy little cell. You'll start drifting off to sleep when the patient in the next bed (who is not as lucky as you and can't sleep) starts tossing and turning – tossing and turning on a bed with a polythene-covered mattress and polythene-covered pillows and creaky bedsprings. It's just loud enough and irritating enough to keep you awake for about an hour. You are just thinking that it will never stop when all goes quiet and you drift into a lovely sleep. I will let you stay asleep for a whole hour. Then I shall put on my high-heeled shoes, the ones with the tips that make a lovely 'clip, clip', walk down the ward, and peep in on you to see if you are asleep – for your own good, of course. You won't know. You won't exactly hear me, but your sleep will be disturbed just enough to make you turn over. The night-time amplification of the rustling and creaking of all the beds as I proceed on my rounds disturbing everyone will do the rest.

Now you will feel a little irritated because you can't get back to sleep. The light seems brighter, and the patient in the next bed can't sleep either and she's put her light on. You will toss and turn. You decide to go to the toilet and come back expecting to settle down, which you do, and fall into the best sleep of the night. A good two hours. Then Shenette starts.

We know about Mary Fryer, don't we? She must creep into the ward at night and waken Seneta.

'Get out of my head, Mary Fryer. Leave me alone. Go away.'

But it is not Seneta's voice that wakens you. No, it is Joan's, telling Senata to shut up and to go back to bed because by this time Seneta is kneeling by her bed praying. So you will pray too and hope that God is listening to your plea for sleep.

He's not. Seneta decides to get up now. She storms down the ward hoping to get a bath. A loud argument follows at the end of which you are not sure whether the noises you can hear are Seneta getting dressed for the day or undressed to go back to bed; by now you are so tired you don't care. So after a second trip to the toilet you get your next long sleep. Let's say three hours.

Now this is the best bit. This is the bit I shall really enjoy. Remember that you are in your deepest sleep. I shall bang the front door. You will turn over in your sleep. I shall bang it again. You'll begin to surface. I shall bang it again. This will be repeated over and over like verse and chorus: you waking and dozing and me banging the front door. You won't know whether you are mad mad (annoyed) or just crazy mad. I'll bring in loud voices – cheery loud voices of people finishing the night shift and others starting the day shift. They are loud because the corridors have an amplifying effect.

It is at this point that you want to add your voice to the cacophony but dare not. You are not in here because they think you are sane. Will angry shouts from a heap of tangled bedclothes help your case? You wonder what words would convey your message. Be careful not to mention God or the devil and certainly not Mary Fryer.

'Oh Christ!'

Now did you shout that out loud or was it in your head?

'Breakfast's ready,' shouts a cheery voice. 'Are you OK?'

'Yes, fine,' you reply through gritted teeth because you might get your discharge today – that is if you can convince them that you are sane. And the fear is that if you stay here one more night, you are not sure that you'll know how to do that.

I hope this will give you some idea of what it feels like to be a patient in ward 101. You see, most of these problems can be put right so easily now that you know about them.

As much as I would like to, I shall not make a return visit to see the improvements.

Yours very sincerely,

Sarah Wainwright

Chapter Five
Happy Families – Not a Card Game

Sharon stepped off the bus carrying her overnight bag. She walked, hugging the high hedge of the suburban gardens towards the house.

'Hi, Sharon. Wait up. Don't go in yet,' a voice called from the shadows.

'Christ, Steve, you scared me to death. What are you skulking here for?'

They hugged briefly.

'I couldn't face going in alone. I need some moral support. You brought a bottle?' he said, looking at the parcel under her arm. 'Yes, me too.'

'So,' Sharon put her bag down, 'are you really going to tell them tonight?'

Steve nodded and took out a pack of cigarettes. Sharon snatched them away.

'Don't be crazy. No need to kill yourself with those things,' she laughed. 'Dad'll do that when he knows.'

Steve smiled in spite of himself.

'And what about you? When are *you* going to tell them?'

'Don't know if I ever will. It's not...'

She stopped speaking as a taxi drew up. They moved together to open the door.

'Hey, you two. Were you waiting for me? How kind!'

Susan struggled out of the taxi. 'Now, that's what I call a caring family.'

Sharon and Steve exchanged looks but said nothing. Steve paid the driver and picked up Susan's bag. Sharon led the crocodile to the front door. It opened before she could ring the bell.

'Oh, you've all come together. Wonderful! The meal is just ready, and your dad has insisted on opening a bottle of sherry.'

'Really?' they chorused.

'I told him not to, but he said it was special tonight – us all being together for once, makes him proud. I know he doesn't say much, but... well, you know...'

They each kissed Muriel on the cheek as they passed into the dining room where Jack was organising glasses. Then Sharon and Steven placed their bottles on the drinks cabinet, which rarely contained alcohol except at Xmas.

'There's a starter on the table, and the trolley is all ready in the kitchen with the main course.'

'Give us a chance to sit down, love,' said Jack, who was sitting at the head of the table and lining up the glasses in front of him. He started to pour.

Muriel took her place at the other end of the table and placed a half-full glass of sherry in front of her.

'How nice this is! All the family together for a change.'

Susan, the youngest daughter, refused the sherry.

Placing her hand on her swollen abdomen, she said, 'Not for me, Dad. Remember, the twins?'

'How could we forget,' said Sharon, the oldest, taking her glass and tasting the amber liquid. 'Look at the size of you. Are you sure it's not triplets? We had a woman in last week who had quins. There's a lot of it about, you know.'

'A lot of what about? Pregnancy?' said Stephen, the middle child. 'You are a fool, Sharon. Of course there's a lot of it about. It keeps the human race going. I thought a newly qualified midwife would know that.'

'Ha, ha. Always the joker. No, stupid, multiple births.'

'And why should there be more than usual?' asked Muriel.

'Well, apart from the heredity factor, there's IVF treatment, which often leads to at least twins and sometimes as many as six or seven.'

'Thank Christ, I'm only having twins. I feel like a hippo now.'

'And you look like one.'

Susan reached over to flip Steven with her serviette but missed and caught Jack's glass; he managed to catch it before it fell.

'Bloody hell! Imagine six or seven like you lot!'

'Did you never think of IVF treatment, Mum?' said Susan, drinking from her glass of water and regretting it. It would make her pee even more than usual.

'Some people's ignorance!' said Sharon, finishing her drink and holding it towards Jack who frowned but filled it nevertheless.

'What d'you mean? Mum could have had it, and she wouldn't have needed to adopt us little darlings. Ever thought of that?'

'Because...' intervened Steven, standing up and walking round the table to pour himself another glass of sherry. 'Because,' he repeated and tugged Susan's hair as he walked back, 'my dear little sister, IVF wasn't an option in the fifties when we were born.'

'And thank the Lord Almighty for that,' said Jack. 'At least we got to choose how many we got.'

'Notice they stopped at three,' whispered Steven in Susan's ear. 'That was because you were—'

Susan pushed him so hard that he almost fell off his chair.

'Grow up, you two. And Jack, I really wish you wouldn't blaspheme so much. You know I don't like it. *And*,' she emphasised the word, 'we seem to be imbibing more than usual too.'

Jack's reply was to walk to the drinks cupboard to take out the bottle of wine that Sharon had brought.

'You never noticed things like that before the new vicar came,' he said, sitting down to open the bottle at the table.

'I'm going to serve the main course before we are all too drunk to eat.'

'One bottle between five, Mum? Come on, lighten up. I've got the weekend off. Susan's going to be tied up soon with the twins, and Steven's actually given up his Saturday evening to spend it with his parents, not to mention his darling sisters whom he loves to bits.' She drained her glass and held it out. 'Nice wine that. Better than altar wine, hey, Dad?'

Muriel began to serve the food from the trolley, which was stacked with plates and tureens.

'I thought we were here to enjoy each other's company. We don't need wine to do that. I didn't bring you up to insult each other either. There is nothing wrong with our new vicar, is there, Steve?'

'He should know,' said Jack, carving from the joint that Muriel had placed before him. 'He's there every Sunday. Sometimes twice.' Jack emptied his third glass and wondered if he should open the other bottle. 'I don't know what he's got. But whatever it is, this family laps it up.'

'Well, it's not wine,' said Muriel.

Steve drained his glass and thought that it was not at all how this evening was supposed to go. He had to tell them tonight, or it would be too late. Sharon got up and walked round the table to stand behind Steven.

'Come on, Steve, there must be a really good reason for you to give up your Saturday night.'

Sharon bent down and spoke loudly near his face. 'We all know that you would much rather be spending the evening with... now, who would you be with?'

'Have you got a girlfriend at last?' said Jack, standing up. 'Well, let's toast to that, everybody? I was so worried. I have to admit. When you used to play that bloody record all the time, I thought you were gay. Oh this bottle's empty. Better get another, hey Muriel, old girl? Got to toast our son's new girlfriend.'

'It seems anything is an excuse to open a new bottle these days, Jack. And I really wish you wouldn't call me "old girl". Did you know about this, Susan? You never said anything when we went to the hospital last week for your check up.'

Susan wished she could, like Sharon, blur out reality with wine on this occasion. She sighed and poured another glass of water, took a sip, and heaved herself out of her chair as best she could.

'Sorry, everybody, but I really have to pee.'

She waddled to the bathroom thinking why he couldn't wait till the twins were born. It was her time now. She knew how much her mum wanted grandchildren. Being pregnant brought her attention, which she enjoyed. It made a change from Sharon boasting about how many babies she'd delivered. She, Susan, was going to have her own babies – something those two would never be able to do. Steven was going to spill the beans. All attention would now be focused on him. Maybe this time it won't be the kind he wants.

Steve pushed Sharon away and went to take the bottle from his dad who was swaying slightly and trying to push in the corkscrew. Muriel made a mental note that this was the second bottle, and she was hardly drinking and Susan not at all.

'Let me do that for you, Dad. You go and sit down.'

'I have something to tell you.'

'Oh, you're not getting engaged, are you, Steve? We haven't even met the girl yet.'

Sharon tried to hide her sniggers behind her hand, but Muriel noticed and so did Susan who was on her way back from the bathroom. They both spoke at the same time.

'Sharon, you know something,' said Susan.

'Shall we eat more and drink less and enjoy the food, which I've spent hours cooking? I'll get the sweet. Perhaps it will soak up some of the wine you have all drunk. Then Steven can tell us his news.'

Susan said, 'If you know something, Sharon, why don't you tell? Looks as though Steve's been struck dumb.'

Steven had opened the bottle and filled Jack and Sharon's glasses. He was now sitting gripping his own empty glass and staring into it as though the words he needed were hidden in there. No joke came to mind to ease the tension on this occasion.

No one touched the sweet which Muriel served. She stood up and, looking them each in the face, announced, 'I'll make some coffee. I think we all need to sober up. And whatever it is, I think you should have told your parents first.' At the word 'parents', Steven thought, *Maybe when they hear what I have to tell them they will wish they had never adopted me.*

'If you don't tell them soon, I will.'

'Shut up, Sharon. You're drunk.'

He jumped up and walked round the table. He was still clutching his empty glass. This was harder than he had thought it was going to be. An angry silence hung over the diners when Muriel returned and poured out coffee for them all. Susan refused hers by pointing to her forthcoming twins.

Steven began, 'I've been…'

He stopped and walked back to his seat.

'Yes, yes, you've been seeing someone. Go on, go on.'

'It's not what you think.'

'I'll say,' said Sharon, reaching for the bottle, 'for God's sake, spit it out.'

Steven opened his mouth to speak, but before he could get his words out the doorbell rang.

'Who in the name of—at this time—on a Saturday night?' They all sat looking at each other open mouthed.

Steven's stomach was churning. The sweat ran down his back, and he wiped his forehead with his napkin. He couldn't even stand, never mind walk to the door.

'Will somebody answer that bloody thing?' said Jack, who didn't trust himself to walk in a straight line.

'I'm not going to wobble there in my condition,' said Susan, smoothing her dress over her bump. *Nobody gives a toss about me anymore,* she thought.

Steve looked as though he would never move again.

'DRING, DRING, DRING.'

Sharon stood up, swayed a little, and said, 'I'll go.'

'Sit down, Sharon. You are in no state to answer the door.'

Muriel rose from her chair, looked around at each of them in turn, and wondered what had become of her family. Striding towards the front door, her anger surprised her. What was happening? She put on the safety chain, opened the door a crack, and snapped, 'Who's there?'

A familiar voice said, 'Sorry to call so late, but I thought you might...'

Muriel didn't know what to do. She couldn't let the vicar in when they were in the middle of a family row. Besides Jack was drunk again, and Sharon could hardly stand.

'It is a bit late, and we're all tired, you know.'

'I do apologise for the inconvenience, but I thought you might need—'

'The thing is, we are just having a family discussion. It's a bit private, a bit, you know, personal.'

Muriel felt a hand on her shoulder and saw Steven's other hand taking the chain off the door.

'It's OK, Mum. Let Mark in.'

'Mark? Who's Mark? No it's the vicar.'

'Yes, I know, Mum. He's the vicar. He's called Mark, and he is the person I've been seeing.'

'Don't look so shocked, Muriel. You knew I was gay, didn't you?' said Mark, closing the door.

'Yes, but, but I didn't—'

Mark put an arm around them both and said, 'Now let's go and have a toast with the rest of your lovely family. Sorry to burst in like this, but I got cold sitting out there in the car, and Steve didn't come to get me at nine like he promised. No, don't get up. You stay there and finish your coffee. I expect I'm a bit of a shock. I bought a bottle of champagne to celebrate our moving in together – Steve and me, that is, of course. Steve told you we're moving to London? Hi, Susan. How wonderful to be having twins. You look radiant, and that's another good reason for champagne. Sharon, you're not leaving, are you? Do sit down and join us in our toast. Steve tells me that you've just passed the finals of your nursing exams. We should toast our newly qualified midwife. Nurses should earn masses. You do a marvellous job for society.' He bent down and whispered in her ear, 'Have you told them your other news yet? I know you'll be happy with Laura.'

He stood up again and addressed the family. 'Let's have some clean glasses for everyone, Steve. Seems like we've all got something to celebrate: Susan's twins, Sharon's exam success, your coming out, Muriel's raising such a beautiful well-balanced family. You too, Jack. You must be so proud of them all.'

Muriel was too stunned to refuse.

Susan thought, *Sod it. One glass can't hurt.*

Sharon was so drunk she no longer cared that Mark had let her cat out of the bag too.

Steven thought that he should have known that Mark would handle it better than him.

'Steve, pour your dad a glass of champagne. He looks a bit shocked.'

Introduction to Chapter Six

How can anybody know

The wringing, wrenching sorrow,

Wrought by that tiny seed?

How can one staunch

The waterfall, wailing and tears?

[Jean Wild]

'Adopted People have had Access to Identifying Documents since 1975.'

The paper shook as Sarah read the headline; her stomach churned. How long had it been since she'd thought about her son? Twenty? Twenty-five years? Did she dare think about him now? Did she dare remember?

She sat down and thought about the day she forgot – the day she made herself forget. She was in a neighbour's house. Her automatic washing machine had broken down, and her friend Doreen had said that she could use her twin tub. So there she was in that cold back kitchen by the big, white sink. She bent down to the red-tiled floor where her family's dirty clothes were sorted into piles (whites, coloureds, and hand wash). She picked up a grubby towel and dropped it into the wash tub. She reached down again for another as though in slow motion. Her body drooped and sagged like a puppet on loose strings. Through the fog in her brain she heard Doreen say, 'Let me do that for you.' Her friend's suggestion shocked her into action. It could not be that Doreen actually meant that she should do her washing. She, Sarah, was the one who was the good housewife. She was the one who did all her work (washing Monday, ironing Tuesday, upstairs Wednesday, upstairs Thursday, shopping Friday) before she had a cup of coffee, visited a neighbour, or took the kids out. She was the one who washed her nets every week and was first to peg her washing out in the mornings. It was her sideboard that was dust free, her kids' toys that were always put away. How dare Doreen suggest that she could do her washing when you could write your name on her windows and other things you would not believe? (Sometimes her husband's tea was not on the table when he came home from work.) There and then she decided that it was will power that she needed. She stood up straight. The fog in her brain started to clear.

'No, thank you,' Sarah said. 'I can do it myself.'

She made herself work quickly and resolved that from then on every time the baby came into her mind she would think about something else. And the power of the human mind is such that it worked. She could not tell you now, all these years later, his date of birth, not the month, not the year, nor the day. What good would remembering do? After all, it had been such an effort to forget. But the article said that adopted people had the right to have access to identifying information.

What if Simon finds me? Sarah thought. *What will I do?*

But she knew exactly what she would do. She would throw her arms about him, and he would know that she was happy to be found. She would try to explain truthfully why she had had to give him away. As the enormity of this possible reunion dawned on her, so did the enormity of the possibility of it happening. She would be easy to find. She had never changed her name and had never moved more than two miles from the house she had lived in when Simon was born.

She tried to prepare herself for what she thought was the inevitable. First of all she recalled with a great effort his date of birth. But then, as the days passed and nothing happened, she began to think the opposite. She did some calculations and realised that he had had ample time to find her. Why would a child who had been given away by his mother ever want to see that mother again? And so Sarah returned to her former solution – that of forgetting. It seemed to be the only way, the best thing for all concerned except, of course, for her. She didn't realise at the time this repression would lead to more depression.

Chapter Six

Searching for Simon

Guilty

Don't look,

At the tiny fingers and toes,

The blue eyes and smudge of a nose.

You'll only remember.

Don't listen

As he breaths, mummers and sighs,

Then wriggles, stretches and cries.

You'll only have nightmares.

Don't feel,

The ache, the pain and the sorrow.

He'll be gone from your life tomorrow.

You'll only be sad.

Don't smell

Hardly there hair and peach soft skin

He was born from your sin

You'll always be guilty.

[Jean Wild]

10 October 2001

I did it! I sent the details to the Adoption Register. It wasn't easy, and it took a long time. Some years ago I heard somewhere (TV, radio, or article in mag.) that the law had changed and that adopted people had the right to trace their birth families but not vice versa. Back then a friend, who was a social worker, sent me information about the Adoption Register. It has two parts, and adopted people and birth families can register to show that they are willing to be contacted by the other party. Then if the birth mother or any other relative wants to be contacted, the adopted person is given the information.

As I said, it wasn't easy. That's why it took me ten years. It is now 2001, and I registered last week. Last year another friend, who is also a social worker, downloaded masses of stuff from the Internet for me. I haven't read it all yet, but I've read enough to get me moving. Some of the case studies were hard to bear. One of my fears, when voiced, sounded stupid: 'What if he's a murderer?' One of the case studies was exactly about that. A woman found that her son was in prison for murder. They were both delighted to have found each other. Previously I had dismissed the idea. *What are the chances of that happening?* I'd thought. But not so. That's why it's not such an easy decision to make although that wasn't/isn't my worst fear. My worst fear is how he will think of me for giving him away. Will he understand that I did it for him? Perhaps if I let him read the 'Crimplene Dress', he will understand. Then there is the father thing. He is bound to want to know about his father. Does that mean that I will have to meet him again?

Recently I have felt very vindictive towards Simon's father. I would like to hurt him, to let him know that he can't do what he did and get away with it. I even went as far as looking in the phone book to find out where he lives, but there are quite a few entries under the same name, and I'm not sure that he lives in the same town.

Well, I finally posted the application to be put on the register. At first I couldn't understand the form. Not that it was complicated, but every time I tried to read it, things got muddled. My brain became fuzzy. The sentences seemed very complex. What did I have to send? (NO PHOTO COPIES. ORIGINAL DOCUMENTS ONLY.) Was it my birth certificate or Simon's birth certificate? I haven't got either. What can I do? They want my marriage certificate. Why that?

The first few times I tried to fill it in but then I gave up. It was too confusing. I was too confused. I couldn't handle it. Finally one morning I decided to do it. I found my marriage certificate, and then, of course, I couldn't remember Simon's date of birth. I say 'of course' because I actually forgot my own son's date of birth, would you believe? Some years ago in the '80s I went to the doctor's and asked her to tell me what date my third child had been born. In fact I had done this in the '70s but promptly forgot it again. The second time I wrote it down. I felt so stupid each time. What kind of mother forgets the date of her own son's birth? The kind who can give her son away, I suppose.

Anyway this time I wrote it down in the back of my diary. Some time later when I inherited my mother's birthday book, I wrote it in– the day and the month, that is. I wrote it on the page for 26 April. It's a book with Bible quotes for each day. My mother was very religious. I'm not. I'm a humanist, but I read the quote all the same. 'Confess your faults one to another and pray one for another, that ye may be healed. The effectual fervent prayer of the righteous man availed much (James 5:16).' Then back to the form. Date of adoption. I can't remember the year. The birthday book has only days and months. I have to find the only concrete piece of evidence I have that I ever gave birth to my son. It was the adoption paper.

This paper had been folded up for years and concealed behind a photograph in a tiny plastic wallet. I was terrified that my husband would find it. Anything that reminded him of Simon brought on an attack of mental rage that led to violence. For years I'd kept it hidden, and I always kept the wallet in my handbag. Eventually when I was divorced, I realised that I didn't have to keep it hidden anymore. So I'd taken it out of its hiding place and unfolded it. It was in danger now of falling apart as it had been folded for so long, but from time to time I could take it out and look at it without fear and acknowledge to myself that I had a third son.

When I met Bill, my present partner, twenty years ago, I told him about Simon; so he has always known. Anyway since my divorce I have lived alone and been independent. I discovered who I was gradually, and I learned to be me. Part of that me was/is a mother who gave away a child and who would one day maybe find him again. Here I was taking the first step after thirty something years. Thirty what years, though? I must find that adoption paper.

I panicked yet again. How could I still keep doing this? I looked twice in the box file marked 'Documents'. It wasn't there. I used to keep it in my handbag. I looked there. My present handbag is quite new. I sifted carefully through all its contents. Not there. I searched the zip compartment. Not there. Think, think, damn it! I moved house last year. Oh my God, it could be anywhere. Think, think. What did I do with my old handbag after I bought the new one? Tool bag! Yes, I converted it into a tool bag. I put some screwdrivers and hammers and things in it. Now, where is it? Richard, my teenager grandson, has been using it to 'do jobs' in his bedroom. Men never put tools away. Ah, it was there under a pile of stripped wallpaper. He is decorating his room. How could I possibly have left it in this? I feel for the inside zip. I open it. I feel the paper. Yes, it's there. I unfold it carefully. I read the date. It tells me the date of the adoption. I write it on the envelope. I put the form in the envelope and post it. Thirty-six years it has taken. How long now if ever??

13 October 2001

I receive the returned marriage certificate plus a statement that it will take about a month to process my application. What does that mean? I may hear something in one month? Am I ready? Will it ever happen?

17 October 2001

Didn't have to wait a month. Reply today. I was really nervous opening the letter. Would I now be able to consider a meeting?

The reply was a total and utter shock. I had not anticipated it at all. 'No - we are sorry to have to tell you that we have no information about your son.' It felt like a smack in the face. Why did I think that he would be looking for me? This was the first step that I had ever taken to look for him. Why would I be so sure that he would be trying to look for me? How stupid!

Well, that was it. Days of disappointment now. More decisions. Do I carry on? If I do, what next? Do I want to carry on? I look at the info again. Too much. Where should I start? I extract some addresses and put them on my desk on the 'to do when I have time' pile.

Tape Julie Walters on TV in film, *My Beautiful Son*, about adopted baby/ man. Beautiful film. Cried buckets. Hide video. I will watch it again. Decide yes, I must do something, but as usual I don't. It's too hard. It's the biggest alone thing ever.

Go to library to do research on photos for the paper I work for. Notice man in the corner who looks like Simon's father. I can't believe it. I haven't seen him for over thirty years. Not sure if it is him. Surprised at my feelings. If it is him, I can't speak. I go downstairs and ask the librarian if she knows the man's name. She has to go and have a look. She tells me the man's name. It's not him. Wondered what I would do if it was. Feel stupid in library now. Staff look puzzled; they must wonder what I am up to.

20 October 2002

A whole year has passed since I wrote in this journal, and I have done nothing about the search for my son. Then I saw this tiny headline in a corner of *The Guardian* on Monday, 14 October 2002:

Changes to Adoption Laws

Thousands of women who gave up their children for adoption over recent decades will get the right to contact them under changes to the adoption law and a 70 million pound boost for adoption services.

What to do? I can't do anything until the law is passed, of course, but what do I do then?

I must decide. I must prepare. Where is that certificate? I can't have misplaced it again. I go in search. Yes, it's where it should be in the document box with the other birth certificates, marriage certificate, divorce certificate, and my will. I may die before I find him. I have never thought that before. I should leave him something in my will. But what? Something else to think about.

The Millstone by Margaret Drabble was serialised on *Woman's Hour* this week. I read it in the '70s and thought it was great. Listening to it on radio, I was astonished to realise that I could hardly recognise it as the same story. The only thing I remembered was that the main character had a baby. The most astonishing thing was that the baby's father's name was the same as Simon's father. He seemed quite nice and amiable, not a bastard like Simon's dad.

25 October 2002

Saw yet another woman on TV who searched for her adopted child. She found him but didn't tell him that she was his mother. She was satisfied to find that he was OK. Will I do the same?

12 November 2002

Started to fill in application form to register my membership to NORCAP (National Organisation for Counselling Adoptees and Parents). I couldn't do it because I couldn't remember Simon's date of birth. I had written it down in one place as 26 March and in another place as 26 April. I couldn't fill in the information about the adoption society either. After all this time I still couldn't do it, couldn't remember. Couldn't, can't, brick wall. I decided to go yet again to the doctor's and made an appointment for 3 Dec, which was the earliest possible.

20 November 2002

I joined NORCAP, and I also joined NPN. It's a support network for natural parents.

Chapter Seven
Breast Lump

11 December 2002

Find lump in breast as big as egg. How could that have grown without me noticing? Impossible! It appeared overnight like a mushroom, no, a toadstool, a poisonous toadstool. Go to French class and on way home call in health centre.

'No appointments till after Xmas,' says receptionist.

'I have to see somebody,' I say. 'I've found a lump in my breast.'

'Come this afternoon at 3:20,' she says.

I start to panic. Go home. Eat lunch. Paint for an hour. And so back to Doc's.

After brief look at lump Doc says, 'OK, I'll fax your details to the hospital. You'll get an appointment in the post. And stop taking HRT.'

'What about a smear test?' I ask.

She says, 'Oh, I haven't got time for that today.' Then, 'No, wait. You had bleeding in May. I'll do it. Make an appointment for after Xmas, and then we'll know what kind of treatment the hospital will administer.'

I go home. John Smith calls to talk about buying property in France. I chat gaily.

'I'm really looking forward to trip in Feb,' I say, but think crazily, *if I'm still here.*

While he's there, the phone goes. It's the doctor's surgery. They have made an appointment for me at the Breast Clinic for Monday 17 December at 1:15 with Doc.

12 December 2002

Woman's Hour. Woman of seventy discovers that she is adopted when applying for birth certificate for new driving licence. She decides to find her mother. She's still alive at ninety in a nursing home. Very bright woman. She also finds a stepsister with whom she has a happy reunion. Don't worry about appointment. Less than eight hours between finding lump and getting hospital appointment. Less than a week between doctor's examination and hospital appointment. I had thought the system was crap. Seems ultra-efficient to me. Or does the speed indicate something sinister?

17 December 2002

Decide to tell only Penny (who is a nurse). Then tell Bill also. In the event, he comes to hospital with me although I really wanted to go alone. His presence seems to make it more serious somehow and me kind of needy.

On arrival at the hospital, I am given a booklet entitled, *About the Breast Clinic*. I am to have three tests: mammogram, X-ray, and an F&A (fine needle analysis) I ask about a biopsy and get a very vague reply, which I don't understand. Lots of waiting and eating sandwiches and chocolate and drinking coffee and Coke. What's the point of healthy eating if this happens?

I am the only person left when the nurse says, 'Well, you must be Sarah Wainwright?'

I leap up and pass young woman in tears coming out of the doctor's room with her mother. The nurse takes my details and leaves me alone saying, 'The doctor will be with you in a minute'. I wait for what seems like hours. I've been in the hospital for four hours, but these few minutes seem longer. I fight back the tears. I know the floodgates will open either way. Relief, if it's all-clear, and fear, if not.

The registrar's words are: 'The mammogram was suspicious; the scan was suspicious; the F&A was suspicious. We don't know if it's cancer.'

The doctor says, 'It could be blah blah, blah rhubarb rhubarb.' He could be speaking Russian. 'More tests. We can do a biopsy now with local anaesthetic. Then we'll have the results in a week.' He talks quickly. It's dark outside. He probably wants to go home. The clinic has overrun by an hour and a half.

I say, 'What does "suspicious" mean?'

He waffles. So far all the doctors have shaken hands with me and told me their names and described in detail what they were about to do to me. But they only deal in facts: 'Just the facts ma'am, just the facts.'

'Yes, do it now,' I say. 'Do it now.'

Doctor leaves and Bill comes in. I cry. Doctor returns with nurse and form. He notices that I am crying and says, 'How you doin', mate?' Really, those were his exact words. He wants *me* to reassure *him*.

I lie down on the bed, and he anaesthetises my breast, cuts it, and then produces what can only be described as a gun. He digs the gun into the cut and fires it four or five times into the lump in order to suck out cells to scrutinise. The nurse repeatedly asks me if I'm all right. Of course I'm not fucking all right. I think, *I've got a lump as big as an egg. This prat is firing a gun into me at point-blank range, and you want* me *to reassure you.*

In between shots, he says, 'Whatever it is, we can deal with it. Don't worry.'

I think, *That's all very well for you to say.*

And he says, 'I know what you're thinking. You're thinking that's all very well for you to say.'

I think. *He's even entering my brain now and reading my thoughts. For Christ's sake, get on with it. It hurts, I'm shit scared, and nothing you do or say will change the fact that you are invading my body.*

The nurse stops the bleeding, puts a pad and plaster on it, and tells me to leave it for forty-eight hours. 'Take a paracetamol if it hurts,' she says.

Will that stop the terror, the sheer terror? I think.

We – I – drive home. Bill has been paralysed with fear. We go into the house, and he breaks down completely. He can't stop crying. I don't want this. I have to hold myself together or let go but not hold him together. Now I have this great sobbing baby in my arms and I can't do it.

I ask him to make pizza and chips. He walks round the kitchen in a daze, picking things up, putting them down, hugging me, and crying, 'I love you, I love you'. I cook the pizza and chips; I nip out and buy wine. He opens the wine and pours two glasses. I look in Louise Hay's book for causes of breast cancer. 'Not caring for self/not being able to give to self/neglect of self.' Well, what a surprise! In the last two weeks, I have helped all my offspring to move house.

Find book about breast cancer written in 1982 in my book case. It says that cancer is systemic, and no matter what they find it has probably spread to other parts. Shock! Horror!!!

18 December 2002

Next Morning Bill is crying all over the place. I tell him that I can't help him; he must talk to someone else, go and see his doctor or somebody. He says that he wants to be there for me, but he needs me to help him. I can't help him.

He makes breakfast and finally leaves. I have decided to ring Penny and Joan. I know that Joan's mother had breast cancer twenty years ago and she's still alive. I feel such a baby.

Think, *If I contact Simon will he think it's only because I've got breast cancer?*

Think, *I'm not in a play. This is real, but it doesn't feel like it. Toothache is real.*

20 December 2002

Waken up feeling drugged. Uncontrollable crying. I know it's cancer. More crying and sobbing. Feel heavy. Get up. Feed cats. Make drink. Go back to bed to read. Read two books that Penny got for me from the library about breast cancer, then Bill rings. He seems more able to cope. I talk about some of the things on my mind. He is very helpful. Millions of what-ifs come to mind, and it all seems bizarre to even think them when I don't even know the results. Well, not officially. Only what I feel. There is only a tiny sliver of hope that it may not be cancer unlike this huge barrage balloon of certainty that it is.

Weather, clear blue sky, bright sunshine, and heavy frost. I'm still in the play except, for the first time in my life, there's no script. My character is definitely a woman with breast cancer, but who knows how to play this part. It's not something like cooking that we learn when we are young. It's not something we learn from role models because other women who have played these parts have done so without an audience or at least a very select audience. It seems that a large part of this role involves keeping it a secret. So do I change it? There's an idea. I could wear a badge saying, 'I've got breast cancer'. This could open up a myriad of possibilities.

When I picked Lizzie up from work last Friday, she was wearing the pink bow for breast cancer awareness. Last year she wore the red one for AIDS awareness.

21 December 2001

Go for sauna with Penny. It feels bizarre walking around naked all day wondering, *Will I have only one breast and a big scar next time?* I've never seen a one-breasted woman in the leisure suite. When I get home Bill is there. We sleep fitfully. Both of us waking in the night and sobbing. I have never felt such fear. I've planned many things in the wee small hours, but this time I'm planning hospital stays, deathbed scenes, funerals, wills, and sobbing – uncontrollable sobbing.

Somehow we get through the weekend. We sit together, holding hands, kissing often, hugging, clinging to each other as though we can hold on to life. As though we can keep each other alive by—by—by what? I don't know. And still the unexpected outburst of tears. They just appear, anywhere, anytime, and I feel a fool.

We read books about breast cancer, possible treatments, lumpectomy versus mastectomy, reconstruction maybe, maybe not, with or without silicone. If I have to have chemo/radio therapy and lose my hair, it may grow back curly. Is that the good news? Lose a breast, win curly hair.

24 December 2002

Today is the first time that I have ever in my memory left a meal uneaten. I can't think. I can hardly move. My stomach feels icy. I'm confused. I walk around in circles. We leave early. The week's waiting has seemed like a year. I feel like a dead woman driving.

Of course we have to wait at the hospital. The waiting room walls are plastered with posters advertising helplines and support groups. I write down the number of a local support group.

'Sarah Wainwright.'

I physically jump as my name is called.

Now, now I'll know.

The surgeon says that he has to do more tests.

'But, but...' I stammer.

He reads the notes more carefully.

'Oh, sorry,' he says, 'the results of the biopsy are still on the computer. I'll go and get them. He returns with a nurse who is introduced to me as the breast care nurse.

He tries too hard to convince me that the lump is benign. He uses the word 'cancer'. He says only because he knows it is on my mind. I refrain from asking him why I had a biopsy. What was he looking for if not cancer?

He would like to remove the lump anyway, he says, so that the pathologist can examine the whole of it. He draws me a diagram saying that he's not an artist. I think of saying that if he is going to perform the surgery then I would prefer it if he was a surgeon.

'It won't take long,' he says. 'You can come in and go home the same day.' I say that I doubt it because it is a very big lump. The nurse nods in agreement. 'Mmmm. Let me take another look.'

Consults diary. 'Come in on Jan 2, and you can go home on Jan 3 or 4.'

He leaves to go to the next patient. The breast care nurse remains and tries to convince me that the surgeon is right and that it is not cancer. I think this is odd. Why would she think that I *wouldn't* believe him?

We now have to get through Xmas. Why am I not elated? What do I know? I've only read a book and looked at a few photos and watched my best friend die two years after having a lumpectomy. I heard the young doctor say to her, 'People don't die from breast cancer.' He was right of course, but she did die from secondaries.

The surgeon's and the nurse's final words were, 'Go away, and have a lovely Xmas'.

It didn't feel convincing. However, we stagger out of the hospital supporting each other as though we've just come out of a war zone. Life goes on, at least for the moment.

Now I have to get through Xmas and the New Year without telling the family and pretending that there is nothing wrong. It seems selfish to tell them now and spoil Xmas and the New Year for everyone.

Xmas Day 2002

Passed as most Xmas days, I think. I was concentrating so hard on keeping in my impending op that I hardly noticed it.

Boxing Day 2002

Everyone goes to sales except me. Peace at last. One week today, and I'll be in hospital. I'm sure it's run of the mill for the surgeon. But not for me. It's *my* breast. I keep feeling the lump half expecting it to disappear as quickly as it came. How could it grow so big without me noticing it? Would it disappear if left alone? What would happen if I didn't have surgery? If it's benign, why does it have to be cut out? Seems a bit drastic. Is it for medical research? The surgeon was quite sure that the pathologist would want to examine the whole lump. Also the book was adamant that a fibrodaema could never turn into cancer. But then if there are cancer cells there, they might already have spread to other parts of the body!!

Just re-read in my journal about the adoption paper and I've lost it again. Where the f—have I put it?

2 January 2003, City General Hospital

At 10:30 a.m. we leave for the hospital. After great difficulty parking we make it to the admittance. The doctor comes and takes me to a bed. It's not for me, he explains. It's just so that he can do the preliminaries. He takes my details, pokes the lump, and takes my blood pressure and more blood. Then to a day room. The day room smells like a canteen on account of the huge mobile food trolley, which contains lunches for the ward.

Finally at three o'clock I am taken to a ward, which is like a private room. I have my own facilities: wash basin and toilet and my own TV. The nurse comes in with my notes and yet again all the same questions. In between the questions, she does things to me. She covers my upper body with stickers and connects me up to a machine. I have no idea why. She does not enlighten me, and I do not ask because I have become so used to people taking liberties with my body I hardly notice. And of course she pokes my lump, which I feel has now become public property. I swear the tea lady had a poke when she brought me a cup of tea. The questions are bizarre:

Last bowel movement? (I hope not!)

Can you walk without a stick?

Do you prepare your own meals?

Do you live alone?

Have you any loose teeth?

And many more.

She finally leaves. I have a visit from the surgeon who, of course, has another poke. Drawing another diagram, he explains exactly what he is going to do. I think he's a frustrated artist. He says he will make the incision near the nipple where the scar will be less noticeable and that he will scoop the lump out from below. 'It's a trick of the trade', he tells me. (Oh goody, I'm glad I'm being done by a real tradesman.) I'm fifth on the list tomorrow. I ask how long will the operation be.

'As long as it takes,' he says. 'I want to do a good job.' (As opposed to me who wants him to bodge it PDQ.) He marks it with a cross. At least they won't cut off the wrong tit, or, to be correct, they will cut off the tit marked wrong. Maybe they should mark it with a tick. After all it is the right tit. Will he tick it after the op?

I settle into room, use TV, read, and listen to tapes. Could be a nice holiday except for the lump poking, blood pressure taking, and, of course, the impending incision. Incision is one of the technical terms I've learned. Apparently it's an elective incision on the right breast. Does that mean that I have chosen to have it?

4 January 2003

I was wakened up this morning to have my blood pressure taken again. Big audience now. Four doctors. Yes, four. They surround the bed.

'May I take a look?' says one. 'Do you mind?'

'Mind?'

Why should I mind? I think. Why don't you announce it on local radio? I'm sure Sam Plank and all his listeners would like to poke my lump, which, by the way, still hasn't grown and still hasn't changed colour. But I lie there mum, and they all watch and wonder at the size, then leave.

The nurse has left my/her notes open and gone out. She seems to have forgotten me. I take a peek. 'Blood test result: unremarkable.' Unlike my lump then.

I went to theatre early and returned to my room early afternoon.

I went home the next day, but I still had to wait a week for the all-clear. I felt really lousy for a few weeks and stupid because I couldn't understand why I felt so awful, confused, and lethargic. Why was I not euphoric after all the agonizing? Then someone told me that one of the side effects from the anaesthetic was that it affected the brain and it could last for weeks or even months. The operation left me with a scar, of course, and colourful bruising, which disappeared; but the scar remains.

I seem to have exchanged the soft lump for a hard lump, which the doctor finds normal. Now I feel that it was all a pointless but painful and terrifying exercise.

I overcame the effects of the anaesthetic and then I found another lump. So I went to the doc's, and she said, 'You know the routine'.

'Yes,' I said, 'but this time I'm not going to have surgery.'

She just looked at me and didn't speak.

I went to the hospital and lay on the couch in the doc's surgery. He poked around for a few minutes and then said, 'OK, where is it?'

'It's he—well, it was, but it seems to have disappeared. It was there. My doctor felt it. It wasn't my imagination.'

'It's OK,' he said. 'It often happens.'

So hopefully that is the end of that story but not Simon's. It felt somewhat anti-climatic, but now I have so much to look forward to. My move to France. And I want to concentrate on my search for Simon, which I hope will bring me real euphoria!

Chapter Eight
Searching for Simon Cont'd

My son

Murderer, mad, mentally ill,

Conservative, cad,

Concealed from me still.

Who will I find?

What will he be?

One thing's for sure

A stranger to me.

His Mother

Frightened and sad, fearfully ill,

Secrets I've had unknown to him still.

Who will he find?

My eyes start to brim

One thing's for sure

I'm a stranger to him.

[Jean Wild]

4 January 2003

The first information arrived from NORCAP. Newsletter dated November 2002. I read it all straight away from cover to cover. It felt weird being part of a campaigning group for 'this'. It still feels as though I am in a story. It's fiction. It's not real. I'm pretending. The newsletters totally and utterly reach my—my what? My empathies. Crying, crying, and crying. One story was about a child called Simon or Stephen who overdosed on heroin. Really scary. Then at the back of the newsletter, a whole page of names of people who have been reunited. One day I may see Simon and his mother Sarah on that page.

There was a small slip of paper stapled to the accompanying letter containing five very important lines: 'It may be worth approaching the Social Services Department/Adoption Agency that placed your birth relative to see if they would consider assisting in a search for the adopted person via a Non Disclosure Agreement. Should you wish to have more information on the agreement i.e. costing and procedure please ring one of our contact leaders on the list.'

A handwritten PS said, 'You will need to purchase a copy of Simon's original birth certificate to ensure his details are correctly entered.' How can I be sure that they are correct when even I his mother can't remember? The PS continues, 'Please ring one of the contact leaders on the enclosed list. Any of them would be pleased to advise you,' and is followed by the address that I was advised to write to.

This was the very first time that I had specific instructions on how to proceed. I can actually contact somebody about my son! This has given me more confidence to keep the appointment with the doctor.

6 January 2003

When the doctor *showed* me my records with a letter from the woman who arranged the adoption, it started to become real. Simon is beginning to feel real. There it all was in black and white – a real letter and a note saying he had webbed feet. I remembered then. And I remembered that Mrs Ramsden had told me that his adoptive father said that he would be a good swimmer.

I could hardly cope with the doctor's kindness and honesty. She talked to me in a non-judgmental way. I wanted to ask more questions but was unable to because I was holding back the tears.

It was only a two-minute conversation, but it felt like a watershed. I can never describe how much it meant to me to see something tangible and to talk to someone about Simon's birth.

I decided to register with NORCAP to initiate a search. I don't know what they can do, but I think they will be able to get some information about Simon for me.

5 February 2003

Time flies yet again. I have now retired from publishing the journal. I am spending a lot of time learning to speak French. I have found a house in Brittany that I would like to buy.

There are so many adoption organisations. I had no idea there was so much help. I feel more validated all the time. I feel less like an outcast, knowing that there are thousands of women who, like me, *dare* to talk about it.

I have decided to go to the NPN AGM, which is on Saturday 26 April in London. How bizarre that that's Simon's birthday! Also I am going to a service called The National Service of Thanksgiving, Reconciliation and Hope, which has been held on the day before Mothering Sunday for the past five years. This year it will be held in Chester on 29 March. I would like to meet other women involved in adoption, but the God bit will be difficult.

25 February 2003

Went to registrar and bought a birth certificate for Simon. It was so easy physically, just a formality. But emotionally it was like reaching the summit of a mountain. My own son's birth certificate! His name and my name, his mother, on the same document. Of course it said 'adopted' at the bottom, and the space for 'father' was blank.

9 March 2003

I wrote that very important letter to Social Services. It took me three days. It was so difficult to write. I must have written it a dozen times before I managed it without making a mistake. Finally I typed it on the computer. I did feel like a beggar asking for crumbs. But he's my son.

12 April 2003

Two things happened yesterday. I read about natural parents of adoptees being possible sufferers of post traumatic stress syndrome, and I went to see a film called *The Magdalene Sisters*. Today I am almost paralysed.

I have re-read what I have written so far in this journal. I did go to the Mothering Sunday Service in Chester. Big mistake. I wanted to cry but was not allowed to by do-gooders who stopped me with their 'wanting to make me feel better'. Why can't people understand that sometimes it is necessary to cry in a safe place? People who stop others from crying do so only to protect themselves from other people's visible pain and to make themselves feel better.

Also I couldn't stand the God/Jesus part. I should have known better, but I genuinely believed the statement that all would be welcome no matter whether one had a god or not. I am not saying that I was not welcome. It is that I have a problem with being in church. Being a Humanist means that I do not have a god, but I do have a moral code. Religious people frequently assume otherwise. Experiencing the church service and seeing the film *The Magdalene Sisters* brought me to thinking how much damage religion can do to the human spirit and how much harm people can inflict on others, especially women, in the name of God.

So it's catch-22 again as usual. Remembering is painful, wearying, exhausting, and as yet unproductive. So why not forget and suffer depression?

23 April 2003

No reply from Social Services. After seeing *The Magdalene Sisters* I felt hurt and traumatised. I was taken back thirty-seven years to the exact feelings and thoughts, and I relived the whole trauma again. For days I felt exhausted and in shock. I cried frequently. I was totally unprepared for this reaction. I wouldn't have thought it possible to re-live such a buried experience, which had happened so many years ago. Even now, two weeks later, it is as vivid as though it was yesterday. I'm not remembering what it was like to hold him or to feed him. I am remembering the pain of the loss and the bodily reactions to that pain. It's as though my muscles and veins and arteries have a memory where my mind doesn't. This is what made me decide to find out what had happened to my letter.

I rang Social Services. After much passing on to others and ringing back and not ringing back and me ringing again I was amazed to get a call from someone who apologised profusely over and over. Even more surprising was that another person phoned to make an appointment *to come and see me* next Friday afternoon, which is the day before I go to London to the AGM of NPN. I have also planned to go to the records office at Kew next Monday. It seems incredible. It is incredible. After all this time I may have something specific to help with the research at the records office.

Finally I feel as though I have emerged from a thick fog of ignorance and invisibility. Am I no longer a person with a secret, a person without rights? I have feelings, thoughts, and memories, which I may now talk about.

It's hard now, but what I realised this morning is that it is going to be even harder. I have noticed that in all the other stories that I've heard or seen on film or TV, the mothers were young, unmarried women. In all cases the attitude now towards them is that they were young and innocent and because of the attitudes prevalent at the time they had no other option.

But what about my story? It's not like that. I was twenty-four and married and I already had two sons. I should have had more sense, but I didn't. I was very naïve, even stupid, and very ignorant. All I knew was how to keep the house clean. I did try to get involved in politics, but that was where I met Simon's father. And that was that.

Simon's father! I wonder if he has ever thought about Simon or thought about trying to trace him. I wonder if he even knows whether he has a son or a daughter. I am very tempted to find out where he lives and to confront him. I have heard stories from birth fathers. All very different from my son's father. All the others seemed to want the baby, wanted to get married to the mother, or at least to have kept the baby. But not Simon's father. The ones I have heard about were all young and unable to take control of the situation. But not Simon's father. He was thirty-six. Just a year younger than Simon is now. He wanted me to have an abortion. He contacted the adoption society. He never came to the hospital to see him. He was married and he had a son.

What will I tell Simon about him?

Friday. What will happen on Friday? I am expecting nothing to happen and to be told nothing except that later this year when the law is changed I shall have the right to know *something*. But what? I have no idea.

Just think, all this time I could have written letters to go on the file and I didn't know. I could have taken photos of him in the hospital, but I was in shock; I was traumatised by the experience and have remained so to this day. It is only during the last two weeks that I have understood just how huge an event this was that happened to me. It *didn't* happen *to* me. I have just realised the enormity of what *I* did. No wonder I had to forget. I couldn't live with myself. I couldn't be that person who had committed such a terrible act.

All this is about me, and that is the tip of the iceberg. What about Simon, his parents, brothers, and sisters? He may have children. What about my children and grandchildren? Everybody will be touched in some way.

24 April 2003

I have been reading the two books that Thelma loaned me again: *The Adoption Triangle* by Julia Tugendhat and *Preparing for Reunion* by The Children's Society. One of the things that I have noticed about all of these case studies is how much information they had and how both adopted people and their parents wrote letters and had them placed on file. What file? Where? I had no idea that there was a secret file. I thought in my innocence and ignorance that all 'evidence' of the adoption was completely inaccessible to ordinary mortals, especially me. I still believe that this was true in 1965, and I felt sure that any information about me, the wicked, shameful, despicable, non-person who committed the offence ('Guilty, guilty, guilty, Your Honour'), all records, all evidence would have been erased. Now, since taking the first few tentative steps, I can hardly believe that gradually not only am I beginning to see and hear and feel and think again, I am being seen, I have become visible, I am being heard, I have become audible, and even my feelings are being acknowledged.

I am thinking, *Why, oh why, didn't I write letters? Why, oh why, didn't I take a photograph in the hospital?* I look back at me then and see someone who was in total shock, and yet I had to get through every day as though nothing had happened. And, of course, for years I suffered the torture from my husband. Why did I never realise at the time why I suffered from depression? Why didn't my doctor realise why I suffered from depression? Save me from professionals and do-gooders!

Now the floodgates have opened. Not just the tears and emotions but the ideas and thoughts. I feel as though I am under an avalanche, and there is no time to deal with it as it comes so fast. I can't think fast enough. It all tumbles in on top of me, and I struggle to write and remember and write and remember and do and read. And what do I expect can happen?

Friday: Social Worker

Saturday: AGM

Monday: Records Office

Maybe nothing. Exactly nothing. Maybe it will have been re-living the suffering for nothing.

In the journal here, I have done two drawings. The first is of myself standing on top of a deep well. I am blindfolded with a caption, 'Me Being Kept in Ignorance Blindfolded and Gagged (and what's more, it was self-inflicted)'. In the well, there is another stick figure of me with the trappings of daily life – school, home, children, pets, and hobbies – with the caption, 'Me Getting on with My Life in Total Ignorance'. At the bottom of the well, hidden in a kind of labyrinth, is a jewel with the caption, 'Hidden under Layers of Silence'.

The second is an attempt to depict Pandora's Box with the caption, 'The Box Is Open'.

The whole exercise may have been for nothing. The saying 'Let sleeping dogs lie' runs around in my head, and yet somehow I can't quite believe that. At the same time, I can't believe otherwise either. It's not like it was thirty-seven years ago. I must find out something. The pain hasn't gone away. It was buried deep. What do I want? What do I hope for? Obviously I want to hear that Simon is OK and that he has had a normal life. Of course I want him to want to see me and of course I want him to like me. I am terrified that he will hate me for what I did, that he will be very angry. And he has every right to be both. If his life is/hasn't been good, then I shall have more reason to hate myself. It will have been my fault. Could I have given him a better life? There are too many possibilities to contemplate. I must be prepared for a variety of outcomes.

Why, I ask myself, have I begun to search now? The reason I didn't search before was that I thought that there was nothing I could do and that I had no right to upset other people's lives especially Simon's again. When the law changed in 1975, I thought that Simon would find me. I wouldn't have been difficult to find. I haven't changed my name, and I have never lived more than two miles from my original address. I thought that if he didn't want to find me, then it was only fair that I should leave him in peace.

Now I feel as though I have had this great big wound covered over by an enormous scab and various events have picked at it. Sometimes little bits have flaked away; sometimes big pieces have dropped off and revealed soft pink fleshy new skin too soft to touch; sometimes thick hard lumps have been lifted, making the scab bleed. The wound has been left unprotected, and I've had to wait for it to heal again. Now it feels as though someone came and ripped off the whole damn scab in one go and left me with an open wound again.

Recently I have thought that maybe Simon didn't find me out of consideration for my feelings in the same way that I have thought about his. The problem is all of this is speculation and all of this may lead to nothing.

Tomorrow I may know all the answers to my questions. OR...

Tomorrow may be a repeat of thirty-seven years ago, and I will be left with a cavernous open wound, which took a superhuman effort to close. Will it close again? Will I be able to close it again? Will I have to close it again?

25 April 2003

Today is the day. I have read both books from cover to cover and sobbed and sobbed. I hope I've learned a lot. The scab is well and truly off, and the wound is wide open. I also read a thick document that had been downloaded from the web two years ago. At that time I couldn't understand it. I was totally confused by it – advice, information, personal stories, help groups, jargon. I didn't know what to do or where to start. Today I looked at it and thought that the first time that I had tried to read it, it must have been in Russian and sometime in the two years it had lain on my desk someone had translated it into English. I could understand it, and, what's more, it seemed to be saying that I had rights. At the very least, I could be treated like a human being with feelings and I wouldn't be judged. Of course Simon will judge me. That's my greatest fear.

I feel prepared. Well, as prepared as anyone who has given a baby away can ever be before learning about the results of her actions. At this moment all I want to know is that he is safe and well. I would also like him to know that if he wants to contact me either by phone or letter or visit, I am open to all and any of these.

I have climbed out of the pit, taken out the earplugs, and removed the blindfold. Now I see a vast desert, which I know to be full of landmines. I have to walk carefully to protect myself and everyone else. If I see an oasis, it may be a mirage. Three hours to go before I hear about my baby of thirty-seven years ago.

The Visit

Anita Jones, social worker, who, I suppose, will be my intermediary, came. So many feelings. Where do I begin? First of all, I am so glad that I read the books that Thelma loaned me. I couldn't have had a better preparation. Anita was lovely, really helpful, and obviously very experienced and skilful. She asked me probing questions, which led me back through the labyrinth of my past. Although I relived the whole experience again, it felt positive and healing and helpful. I realised that I hadn't really visited that place before with a person with whom I could be truly honest, even to myself. I am getting used to saying 'my son Simon'. How does a mother put herself into the position of finding those words hard to say?

We – Anita and I – talked about so many aspects. She seemed to know all the areas and topics that are appropriate.

Many times I have been asked, 'How many children do you have?' I have always replied, 'Two'.

How could I deny his existence? But how could I say, 'Three, but I gave one away'?

I couldn't have said that because I couldn't believe that I had done it. I am a woman, a mother, who gave away her baby. I have never put myself in a position where I could hear negative comments from others; no need to do that at all. I can judge myself and make negative comments.

I told Anita about all the stories that I had read about birth mothers who were 'young, teenage, unmarried girls'. I don't fit into that category. I don't think that I have ever fitted into any category. I've always been a square peg in a round hole. I told her that I felt very guilty about the 'affair'. It seems that having a son adopted is 'punishment enough' for having an affair. However, my husband made doubly sure of that by inflicting physical and mental cruelty for the rest of our marriage. And just for good measure, I am expert at continuing my punishment. I have given myself a life sentence. I explained to Anita that it was a choice between the two sons I had and my unborn baby.

And I never realised the cause of my depression. How stupid was I?

And the father? What was his punishment? I really would like to talk to him. Will I feel able to soon?

Anita stayed for two hours. I couldn't believe that it was happening. She told me that a search could be possible and that if Simon is found I may be able to communicate with him through an intermediary and tell him that I would like to meet him. I would dearly love to meet him, but to know something, anything, about his life would be good.

So I'm real. My son is real. I have allowed space in my body to feel and experience the past in order to enable me to live the reality now and take action. The fear of being treated as I was thirty-seven years ago by officials and society is receding, and I am gaining confidence to take control, to take action, to ask questions. It feels so good. It feels right.

26 April 2003

I went to the AGM of NPN in London.

What an incredible experience it was! I was in a roomful of birth mothers and adoptees all willing to speak openly about their thoughts, their experiences, and their lives. They were all laughing and crying together; they were feeling safe because no one was judging. All of them knew what it was like, is like, and always will be like. There was empathy. No judging, no patronising, and no advice giving. Only good, sound information if needed. I learned a new word: 'relinquished'. I'm not sure that I can use it about myself, but it certainly feels better than 'gave away'.

Three adoptees spoke about their feelings and experiences, which were followed by questions and answers. It was agreed by all that the exchanges between the two groups were useful to all.

Marion Hancock talked about her book, *Searching for Oliver*. I wanted to ask her about publishing, but there was such a long queue of people waiting to speak to her that I gave up.

Marion Hancock said something like, 'It's like peeling the layers from an onion'. If only it were that easy, I thought. It's a good metaphor; or is that a simile? Onions make you cry. No, that's not true. Onions make your eyes water. Onions make tears stream down your face. But onion tears are not attached to feelings, are they? Not like the ones produced from your inner core when your whole body becomes one huge sob and your shoulders heave and you feel it will never stop. It never really stops. Sometimes you find the strength. You have to find the strength to stem the flow, because, if you don't, you would cry yourself away. Bodies are 90% water, aren't they? I think I may end up as a lake of tears – no body, no bones, no skin, just tears, each sob sending out waves and each sigh sending out ripples.

28 April 2003

Went to the National Records Office. I learned how to use the birth register on microfiches. I must go again to search for Simon's in the year 1966 from the January quarter because his adoptive parents may have kept his name or maybe kept 'Simon' as a middle name.

17 May 2003

I discovered later that there is a register called the 'Adoption Register', and it is not in London. This is all very confusing. I think about visiting the place where it is kept, but I'm not sure what information I need. All I can do is to look through the records to find a boy born on 26 March 1965 in Hampshire or registered in Worcester. I don't know whether the Adoption Register records births of adopted people or the adoption details or both.

My social worker came again, and I forgot her name. How can I remember her name when it took me thirty years to remember my own son's? Anyway Anita came again yesterday. I wasn't psyched up for her visit. I kept forgetting that she was coming. She should have come on Wednesday, but she changed the appointment to Friday afternoon. I knew she'd be tired after a hard week. I know all about social workers' stress. I have too many friends who suffer from it. I can empathise with them as a friend, but I resent being a client on the receiving end.

I was right. The first thing she told me was that she'd had a hard week. I immediately felt guilty and worthless being the last client on Friday at five o'clock at the end of her horrendous week; she was going on to Manchester when she left me, which was another hour's drive. At the beginning of the interview (that's what it felt like: 'an interview') she also told me that this would be her last visit. So much for her being an intermediary!

Maybe all this made me cautious. I knew I didn't feel comfortable. She told me the facts in a kind of businesslike way. She had a letter in her hand, which she said would explain the situation. It was all very official and had the feeling that she was saying, 'This is the end of our relationship'.

She can't search, but NORCAP, or some other agency, can as long as they sign a non-disclosure agreement. She brought me some information from my personal file. Who does it belong to, this file? It contains all this information about me, Simon, his adoptive parents, and, for all I know, Simon's father, and none of us are allowed access to it. Talk about Kafka. Is it any wonder I spent my life being depressed?

Anita held this letter and the sheet of information in her hand for the whole of the interview. I was close to tears many times but held them back. I no longer felt safe with Anita. I had thought that I was ready to move ahead.

I had watched a video of the film, *The Other Mother*, the evening before, thinking that it would help. It did in a way, but it also made me realise how complicated everything is. And again I was not a young unmarried mother like the ones I'd heard about who had their babies dragged from their arms while they were screaming to keep them. That wasn't me, isn't me. What does it look like to other people? What will it seem like to Simon when he reads if he ever does, 'Mother was married with two children and had an affair with a married man who also had a son'? That's what Anita told me it said in the file. Of course it's true. 'The facts, ma'am, just the facts.'

What it *doesn't* say is how I felt, how I was desperately unhappily married, how I thought his father was a way to a better future – 'an affair'. That's rich! We met a few times and had sex once. He had already started seeing someone else when I found out I was pregnant. I later noticed that she also became pregnant. And I remembered again yesterday that it was Simon's father who arranged the adoption. He made me an allowance of five pounds a month to compensate for my loss of earnings up to the birth. Everybody knew. My family knew, of course, and my husband made sure that his family knew, and his brother made sure that the rest of the town knew. I suppose that was part of my punishment knowing that everybody knew and having to go about the town as though nothing had happened.

I wondered if there had been anything in the file about Simon's father. Anita said that she thought there was. She had said that she would have another look and let me know. I told her that I had thought of contacting him. She asked me if he still lived in the area, and I said that I thought it was likely. I realise that if I ever do meet Simon that he will want to know about his father. I have always been afraid to look for him, but maybe I should do it. After all he will be… He was thirty-six in 1965, so he will be over seventy now. I think I have to try to find him. There are so many questions that I would like to ask him.

Oh dear! What a mess all this is! Why didn't I fight to keep Simon? Why didn't I pretend? No, that wouldn't have helped, would it? All this mess is because of secrecy. Does the truth hurt?

The truth never hurt anybody.

'The truth hurts, doesn't it?'

The truth will out.

'It's too late to change the past.'

It's never too late!

All these dictums running round and round in my head. At least I can be honest from now on.

I said to Anita, 'Shall I read the letter now while you are here or shall I wait till you've gone?' I don't remember her answer, but I read it while she sat in silence – the letter of facts, of course, and the information from the file.

What an upstanding, self-righteous couple they were/are on paper. I hope for Simon's sake they were not as self-righteous as they were made to look in the file. I hope it was just to satisfy the adoption society. Balancing his adoptive parents against his birth parents, it couldn't have looked worse. Two adulterers against two Christians who were unselfish foster parents, and very upstanding members of the community being Sunday school teachers too. My heart sank. The words described two soulless, unfeeling, unerring automatons. That's all my prejudice coming out. I hope for Simon's sake that they were loving and light-hearted and that house was full of fun and laughter and love, which the home I would have given him could never have been.

And she had typed the wrong date of birth at the top of the information.

18 May 2003

I have just re-read the whole of my journal. Where does this leave me? I still feel helpless, more confused than ever, and paralysed. I said to Anita that I would take some action. Now that I have opened Pandora's Box instead of trying to close the lid, which is not only impossible but would lead to depression, why not have a plan of action? I will write a list of things that I can do. There are so many things that I could try. I start to write, and even as I compile the list I feel guilty. I don't know whether I am doing it to find Simon for his sake or just to make myself feel better.

I have no right to feel better. The crime I committed is punishable by life. Early years of Christian indoctrination coming through here. No need of a judge and jury. I can be both. Judgement: guilty as charged. And punishment: sentenced to a lifetime of mental torture. Now that my husband isn't around to inflict it, I can inflict it on myself.

At this point there is a sketch of a newborn baby and what looks like a plant torn out of the ground with roots dangling bare.

14 July 2003

Returned from France last week after five weeks away in Brittany and in Macon. I have bought a house in Brittany, and I am planning to live there for at least six months. I have about ten weeks to sort out my affairs and to let this house before I leave. I have set the deadline. I suppose I work better with a deadline. Now I am trying to connect with Simon's story. It still feels like a story that is happening to someone else. I thought that the armour was well and truly penetrated in May, but it's not so easy. I've kept it locked away for so long that it is easier to cover the wound than to open it up again. Talk about mixed metaphors – about as mixed as my confused thinking. I am now about to start the list that I wrote in May.

Number one: Contact NORCAP

Or maybe visit the General Register Office Family Records Centre Middleton St London EC1 1UW, Angel tube station, Tel: 017046569824

Opening times: Mon 9:00 – 5:00; Tues 10:00– 7:00; Wed 10:00 – 7:00; Fri 10:00 – 7:00; Sat 9.30

31 July 2003

I have made great strides, and everything is moving very quickly. I suppose this is because absolutely nothing was possible for so many years, and I really believed that unless Simon found me I couldn't do anything. Now each move I make seems colossal and achieves so much. It's such a shock to talk over the phone to people who are non-judgmental and can actually help.

I wrote a long letter to Simon and sent it to Anita to put on 'the file'.

'The file' sounds like a criminal record. It feels like it.

The File

Why oh why, can't I espy

The secret document.

It's not a lie, I can't deny

My child away I sent.

Lots of eyes have read

'Bout you and me, my son

Oh say what right have they,

When, I your mum, have none?

Dear Simon,

This is the most difficult letter that I have ever written. You must have so many questions, and I would like to be able to answer them all.

I imagine the first one would be why have I waited all these years to write. The answer is that I believed that I had no right to information or access to you. I didn't know to where I could write or request information. It was so difficult to continue with my life after relinquishing you that the only way I survived was by using mind over feelings and erasing everything from my mind, which I expect leads to the second question: why I did it and how could I your mother surrender you my son for adoption.

The answer seems trite. I knew it would be the best for you. Yes, I was married and already had two sons. Yes, I did have an affair with a married man – your father. I believed that we had a future together and that I would be able to leave a bad marriage. I was very foolish. It is difficult to imagine what it was like forty years ago, but believe me when I tell you that I saved you from much suffering. I was severely punished for my actions, and the only way I could protect you at the time was to surrender you for adoption.

I hope for forgiveness from you as, believe me, relinquishing a child for adoption commits a mother to a life sentence.

I have many questions for you. I want to know that you have been looked after by your adoptive parents. I was assured that you were a very wanted baby by good people who already had an adopted daughter.

I was informed that you would be told that you were adopted. I hoped that when the law changed in 1975, you would find me. One of the reasons that I didn't try to make contact before was because I thought that since you hadn't contacted me you didn't want to know me. Then I read about the adoption triangle and discovered that there could be many reasons. So now I have put my name on the contact register and done as much tracing as I can.

All of which has lead to this letter which was supposed to be brief.

I would love to know how you are now and what kind of a life you have led. Are you married? Do you have children? But most of all, I want you to be happy.

Well, I am here and hoping, at the very least, to have some news about you. I would be delighted if you wanted to contact me. I would love to meet you. I will agree to whatever you decide.

I never stopped thinking about you.

You have always been near to my heart and always will be.

Love for ever,

Your mother

I wrote the letter, and it took a couple of weeks for me to get around to posting it. Then the same day I rang a researcher on NORCAP's list. I had been trying to get to grips with all the info again and was working through documents and leaflets to decide the next step. My first thought was to go to the family records office in Middleton St to do it myself, but then I thought, *No. The file is there with all the information. I can't have access to it but NORCAP can.* I rang them, and I spoke to a woman called Shirley who was very helpful. Yes, they could do the search. All I had to do was fill in a non-disclosure agreement with NORCAP and Social Services. She asks for a letter from Social Services and she sends me the document, which I fill in immediately and post. The letter says that it usually takes three to four months. I can't believe that it will be so quick. I decide to wait until I know what is going to happen before I let the house and book my ferry to France.

How ironic it would be if I discover that Simon is living nearby and I am moving to France! Or what a quirk of fate, if he already lives in France! It still doesn't feel real. I feel as though I am in a play. Does this play have a final act? When the curtain goes down, will everything have ended happily ever after? Or will it be one of those plays where everything is left up in the air with the audience left to add their own ending? In this case, neither the players nor the audience have the power to change the script. Perhaps that's why it feels like a play. I am not in control; someone else is writing the script.

9 August 2003

I have been looking for the video of a film that I taped about adoption. I watched *My Beautiful Son* again last week and then I wanted to watch the other one. Not only could I not find it, I had forgotten the title. Then I remembered that I had loaned the video to Anita, my social worker. I rang her to ask her the title. Also I wanted to tell her that I had signed a non-disclosure agreement and ask her if she had put my letter to Simon in 'the file'. Although I rang at least three times and left two messages, she didn't ring back until Thursday when I was out. She said that she would not be back in the office until next week. I have just found the title of the film in my journal. It is called *The Other Mother*.

6 April 2004

I can't believe the date. I moved to France on 15 October 2003. From then till now I have tried many times to retrieve the above-mentioned video. No result. I spoke to Anita at least once before I left England, and she promised me faithfully that she would return it before I left England but she didn't. I wrote her a letter and asked her to return it. No reply. A friend contacted her in January and offered to pick it up and bring it over to me as she was coming for a visit. No response. Then in March I rang her again. No apology. She seemed quite unconcerned and said, 'Oh well, you know what it's like. You intend to do it, then you forget.' I gave her my friend's number as she had offered once again to collect it from Anita's office and post it to me. Still nothing. Zero. Zilch. Next month it will be just one year since she borrowed it from me. Why can't she understand that it is very important to me?

Up until 7 February I had heard nothing from NORCAP. I really didn't expect to as I thought it was impossible to find my son. But on that date NORCAP wrote to me to say that the reason that I had heard nothing was because they had *done nothing as I hadn't paid*! I had sent a deposit as was suggested in their instructions, which also told me to wait until I heard from them before sending more money. Apparently they should have sent me a research form and a request for payment. They now suggested that I send three post-dated cheques, which I did immediately.

Weeks passed. Nothing again. Not that I expect anything to happen now because except for the two visits from the social worker nothing has really happened. I rang NORCAP and left a message. Nothing. I rang frequently until I got a real person to speak to. I explained. 'Oh yes, we have been waiting for the cheques to clear. The cheques have cleared now, and we have appointed you a researcher.'

Why, in God's name, didn't they tell me all this before? I would have paid one cheque up front.

I even got a letter to confirm all this. That was the good news. The bad news is that Simon has a very common surname, which means that the search is going to be difficult or even impossible. Surprise, surprise. Am I the only person who experiences all the glitches and setbacks? All the stories I have read are full of praise for the agencies and services. I am grateful to NORCAP and Social Services but can honestly say that the help I have received has been very hit and miss. I am going to the AGM of NPN in April. I hope it will be as positive as last year.

David, my oldest son, and his second wife, Christine, came to see me in January to tell me that they were planning a family after David's vasectomy reversal. As the success of the vasectomy reversal seemed doubtful, they told me that they were preparing to adopt. I tried to keep my opinions on adoption to myself. I handed them newsletters from NPN and NORCAP and books about adoption. David appeared very interested then suddenly said, 'Somebody told me that you had a child adopted. Is it true?'

I said, 'Yes, but I thought you knew because your father told you when you were small.'

He said, 'No, he didn't tell me. I received an anonymous letter some years ago telling me that you had a baby, which was adopted, and that he was living nearby.'

I said, 'I think that is impossible, but maybe it said that his father was living locally.'

He said that he had shown the letter to his brother Matthew. (I was going to write 'my youngest son' but he isn't, is he? Simon is my youngest son.) Matthew had said that he knew about it, and it would be best to say nothing.

So I told him all about my search and everything that I had done so far. I said, 'I have written four letters, one for each of you, and I was saving them until I was near to finding him. I will give you yours now.' I gave them the letter. He read it and said, 'It's just a note. I thought it would be longer.' I suppose he expected explanations, and all he got was copy of Simon's birth certificate and a brief note saying that I had begun a search.

I told him about NORCAP's AGM, which was going to be held in London. They said they may come.

I decided that day that the first person to have an explanation should be Simon himself. I also thought that maybe I would never get the chance to tell him anything.

15 April 2004

Today I received a letter from NORCAP with an update on their search for Simon. My researcher has drawn a blank at the Family Records Centre and the Adopted Children's Register. She is going to return to Social Services for more information in the hope of getting details of his adoptive parents. I began this search with little hope, and now even that is lessening daily.

29 September 2004

So much to write about. Where to start? First of all the AGM of NPN was brilliant. Very moving. I met very interesting people and was able to be my real self. I did not feel guarded in speech – 'Yes, I have three sons', and so on.

There had been a letter in the NORCAP newsletter from a woman who had been married when she had her son adopted and I felt I could perhaps write my story for the newsletter too. However, when I was in Bath for the AGM, I was describing my feelings about not being a young unmarried mum who had had a child taken away from her when I overheard a woman behind me say, 'She wasn't a young woman. She was twenty-five. I think that was terrible. She was old enough to...'

So I wrote the following letter to NPN:

Dear NPN,

I joined NPN and NORCAP at about the same time. I was only just beginning to remember after almost forty years of actively forgetting. So it wasn't surprising that I was delighted to discover... Well, what did I discover? Too much to take in at first. But it was a forum where the unmentioned was spoken about and for the first time I realised that maybe, just maybe, I could talk about my own story.

For years I have denied my real self. Recently I began to recognise who I really am. I am a woman who gave birth to three sons and gave one to another family to adopt. Not many people who meet me know that.

I have attended the last two AGMs of NPN. What a relief to find myself amongst people with whom I could be open! No need to guard every word. But... er... not quite. You see I kept hearing other women's stories, and they were all very similar to each other but not to mine. They were all young and unmarried when they relinquished their babies. Now this is where I begin to retreat again. Maybe I have to forget for another forty years what I did, and then it won't matter because I shall be dead and buried. As I was considering this as a real option I read the story of a woman who is braver than I.

In the last edition of the Newsletter, Josie told her story about how she was married but not to the father of her child. At last, I thought, at least there is one woman whose story is similar to mine, and I began to write a letter. However, before I could post it I attended the AGM in Bath. I was just about to tell someone that I was pleased to read this story and that I was twenty-five when my son was born when I overheard another woman say, '... And I said, how could she? How could she give her own child away when she was twenty-five? I mean it's not as though she was a young girl, is it?' I stopped in mid-sentence. I've said it myself! How could a mother give up her baby? But the point is this: I have spent thirty-eight years judging myself, and I thought that I had found a safe place to be accepted and not be judged. When I tried to explain to her, she said to me, 'Why couldn't you pretend it was your husband's?' – the same words spoken to me by the sister thirty-eight years ago in hospital.

Fortunately I feel stronger now and realise that I have to be prepared for negative comments that I have been hiding away from all these years. I have to face myself, I suppose. I am searching for my son, and I have to be prepared to be judged by him. Ultimately he is the most important person in the equation, and I have to be prepared to answer any question that he may ask.

I also wrote about the Mothering Day Service, 2003, in Chester.

I was apprehensive about attending the ceremony for all the obvious reasons. As a Humanist I was afraid I would have problems with the religious aspect. After reading that everyone would be welcome no matter what their religion was or even if they had none, I decided I would take a risk.

I knew that I would cry, but I thought it would be a safe place to do so and actually looked forward to the service. Lots of women would probably be crying like me, and I wouldn't have to explain why I was crying, or worse, have to stifle the waterfall that had been waiting to flow for so many years.

So I went. After having a cup of coffee, I went into the church and sat as near to the back as I could. As soon as the service began, I started to cry. A woman behind me was most disturbed by my tears and was very concerned for me. She wanted to comfort me and asked me to sit by her. She finally said that she was the vicar's wife and asked if I would I like to go to the vicarage. 'NO, NO, NO,' was what I wanted to shout. 'Leave me alone, let me cry.' But the moment had passed. I listened to the rest of the service out of respect for the participants who had obviously put in a great deal of effort, and then I rushed away.

Sue Boon, who was the editor of the newsletter, wrote this below my letter:

'Thank you, Sarah, for sharing your thoughts with us. Firstly, may I reassure you that NPN is indeed somewhere where you can share your thoughts and feelings. Our main attributes are that we are a confidential and non-judgemental organisation set up in the first place in order that birth parents could share their feelings and stories with others in a similar situation. I believe that you have had a very unfortunate experience so far with NPN. Perhaps you would like to write your story for the Newsletter so that we can all share it with you. Also, if you wish to talk to someone, please call any coordinator (unfortunately we don't have any in France) or any trustee. All the phone numbers are in the Newsletter. Perhaps other members would like to share their thoughts with Sarah either via the Newsletter or directly to her. (I will be pleased to pass on any correspondence if you send it directly to me, the Editor.)'

Also in the same Newsletter there was a short article about my move to France, which read

(There are so many books on the market and programmes on TV about moving to France and all the problems people have with French builders [and I have had lots of those] that it seems old hat now. So I will try to put a different slant on it.)

'I don't remember making a decision to move here. It happened gradually. First of all, when I was nearing retirement age, I decided that I would like to have a really interesting project. I had always wanted to learn a foreign language, and French seemed to be the most logical one to choose since I had studied it at school albeit reading and writing and very little speaking. I had long envied people who had lived in other countries, but I thought that although I couldn't do that I may be able to spend long periods travelling, perhaps in a camper van, around France.

So I joined a French class. For a number of years this class was the highlight of my week, and I made some very good friends. Over the years I met people who had lived in France, people who had holiday homes in France, people who were looking to buy in France, and people who had bought and sold again in France. Soon I found myself taking *French Property News* and devouring every word. Then came the Internet sites. I spent hours on the Net printing out pictures of houses I liked the look of. I went to property exhibitions in Birmingham and London. I drove around France visiting *immobiliers* (estate agents) who showed me monumental ruins, many of which I fell in love with; but common sense and/or the bank balance overruled.

My second plan was to spend a month here and a month back in England. This seemed eminently sensible as at the time I had a small publishing business, which produced a free paper every two months. This idea would work well, I thought.

Eventually I found the house I wanted to buy and to which my common sense and bank balance did not object. It had the three things that estate agents tell you are the most important: location, location, location! I travelled back and forth every month for six months whilst jobs were or as was most often the case not being done on the house. I liked being here so much and, as I was sixty-two, I thought that it was time I should retire. I decided I would try living here for six months. So I let my house in England, sent over as many belongings as I could afford in a removal van, and followed a few days later in my car with my two cats. After a few weeks it seemed easier and more logical to buy a French car, apply for a *carte de sejour* and my *cart vital* for health purposes. Well, my six months are up, and I feel very much a permanent resident here. England has become a place I visit for holidays.

Life in France is both very different from life in England and very different from what I expected. I live deep in the countryside – something I could not afford to do in England. My nearest neighbour is 150 yards away. I am surrounded by fields. My house is the only one in the lane, after which it turns into a track and leads to a field. My nearest farmer has a herd of beef cattle and a herd of dairy cows. He has just planted two fields of maize, one in front of my house and one at the side. I found a salamander behind the barn under a rock, and there are lizards in the barn wall. Every night and early morning I hear an owl hooting, and this morning I heard a cuckoo for the third time.

I live alone, and people ask me if I am afraid or bored or lonely. The answer to all these questions is a definite 'NO'. People here don't lock their cars. There is very little crime and no traffic problems. The only sounds I hear are the wind in the trees, the birds singing, and the cows mooing. If I hear a vehicle, it is the postman, a visitor, or the farmer on his tractor. I came here with high hopes of spending a great deal of time painting and writing. I have managed some of both activities but not as much as I expected. The reason being that there is so much to do. I have lots of visits from friends and neighbours and many invitations from others. There are amazing concerts to attend with world-class musicians. I love dancing, so I frequently go to the many Fez Noz (Breton folk dances), and there are tea dances and balls every weekend. One of the distinctive social events is the communal meal. They are held in the Salle de Fetes (village hall) and are five courses long with a different beverage with each course. The food is served at table with 200–300 people attending. So I am neither bored, lonely, nor afraid.

And I haven't mentioned the garden. I have a field bordered on two sides with poplar trees and one side with oak trees; the fourth is waiting for me to decide what to plant. As I spent twenty years living in an upstairs flat looking at a brick wall, I am delighted to be able to see nature all around. I can just see the River Rance at the bottom of the valley, and on the other side of the river I can see Mérillac Church. I have a huge lime tree in front of my house, which provides protection from the wind in winter and shade from the sun in summer. I had intended to cut a small patch of grass to sit on in the summer and leave the rest for the farmer to cut twice a year, but I have discovered the joys of gardening. If the weather is fine, I spend most of the day lifting large stones, wheeling barrow loads of gravel or soil and cutting more and more of the field to make a lawn. Another important activity is trying to fulfil my first objective, which, if you remember, was to learn French. I have been very fortunate in finding a French class with a marvellous teacher and wonderful classmates. I attend two and a half days a week, which is necessary when one is losing brain cells daily. Now I have friends from Turkey, Kosovo, Brazil, Senegal, and the Congo, and the class is a laugh a minute.

I try to keep a journal, but I am so busy living that I have little time to write about it. I do try to log my thoughts on loneliness and solitude and freedom and such. I am making time to update progress on the search for my son. I have kept a logbook since I allowed myself to remember.

So if you fancy a holiday in the country, contact me. I have lots of beds for visitors. I don't charge, but you would have to do your own cooking or eat out, which is amazingly cheap and delicious.

29 September 2003

I received two letters after the publication of my letter from women telling me that I am not the only one who was not a young unmarried mother. We could start a new organisation or perhaps a section of NPN called 'Not young unmarried mothers who gave up their babies for adoption'.

I have also met a woman who lives here in Brittany called Barbara who has been exceptionally hospitable to me. I discovered that she too gave away a child for adoption – her third child. She was married at the time but not to the father. Barbara told me how her daughter came to find her and that she had even been to this house last summer before I moved in. That felt very weird. We have talked at length and I feel – what do I feel? – perhaps not so wicked or not wicked at all.

I have this strong desire to write to Simon. I will get my file out, read the letter that I sent when I first found out about the file, and then I will write another letter. I feel I have to counter the negative stuff in that file to make it more balanced.

I have been thinking of writing more to Social Services to be put on the file. But would it get there? Anita still has not returned my video. Thelma sent her a letter yesterday. She sent me a copy by e-mail, but I was unable to download it. My computer is broken again. Perhaps tomorrow it will be repaired and I can read it then.

On 14 July I had a letter from NORCAP saying that they had located Simon's parents. This seemed like a giant leap forward. They asked me to send a short biography and a photo. How do you write a short biography at sixty-three and what is the photo for? I did ring up to ask and was told that it was not to be passed on to anyone but was just for the intermediary to have an idea of the kind of person I am! They also told me again that as he has a very usual surname, it would make it difficult to trace him. But the amazing thing is that I was told that there are no first names on the adoption certificate. I find this hard to believe as I thought that this was a legal requirement. I plan to phone again tomorrow to ask about this.

Why are there no first names on that certificate? Very strange.

8 November 2004

About two weeks ago I rang NORCAP. I had to ring three times before I got to speak to someone who could talk to me. That was understandable as the two previous weeks *Woman's Hour* had devoted time everyday to the 'topic' of adoption, and I expect NORCAP had been inundated with phone calls. I was amazed, delighted, and terrified to hear that a letter was in the post. My details/case had also been sent to an intermediary, which I assumed had been done weeks ago. I asked my question: why were there no first names on the certificate. I was told that there would have been a name but only one; that would have made it more difficult because two or three names make the search much easier.

So I wait for the letter. It arrives. The letter tells me the name (Janet) and phone number of my intermediary. It asks me to give her time to read my papers and then to phone her. The letter arrived on Monday 1November, and I rang on the Friday following. I had a long talk with her. She read out a letter, which she was going send to Simon's parents. Apparently that is how it had to be out of respect for the parents. Fair enough. She said she would enclose a form for Simon to sign to say that he had read the letter which his parents were asked to show him. Janet had explained that even if the letter came back signed it wouldn't necessarily mean that Simon would have read it. She also cautioned that we/I wouldn't automatically receive a reply. Obviously some adoptive parents didn't want to hear from birth parents. She said that if we didn't get a reply within a month that she would send a further letter but that that might be difficult as by then it would be getting near Xmas which was always a difficult time. I would receive a copy of the letter. She told me she would post it tomorrow Saturday, 2 November.

What did I feel? I allowed myself to feel a tiny twinge of excitement. At last maybe, just maybe, I would get a result of some kind, even if it is just to say, 'I don't want to know you, Mother.'

People repeatedly ask me why I am doing this. In fact I ask myself the same question all the time. The answer is that I want to know that he is OK. I want him, Simon, to know that I love him, and if he needs me in any way I will be there for him. Of course the best outcome would be to have some kind of relationship with him. The worst will be no response at all. I was prepared for the worst.

15 November 2004

What Actually Happened

I returned home on Monday at 6:30 to a house full of guests from England. They had let themselves in and lit the fire and made a pot of tea. Before I drank my tea I listened to my phone messages. There were three. The room was buzzing with conversation.

My friends, whom I hadn't seen for a long time, were excited about seeing me and my house in France. I was excited about seeing them and knew they would love the house and the field. My partner Bill, who lives in England, had just arrived too, and we were all talking at the same time.

There was this message that I was trying to listen to: '... Some news for you.'

I think I said aloud, 'It's Janet, Janet. I'll ring straight away.'

I pushed one button to return the call.

Me: 'Hello. It's Sarah here. You—'

Janet: 'Did you get my message?'

Me: 'Yes. You have some news for me about Simon?'

Chapter Nine

Happy Families Not a Card Game Two

Steven slammed the taxi door, which had brought him from the Opera House where he worked in the bar. As he ran upstairs he imagined the feel of the mattress greeting his tired limbs. Mark was standing in the hallway of their flat holding out the phone.

'It's your sister, Sharon.'

Steven grabbed the phone which Mark was holding out to him.

'What's up, Shaz? It's 2:00 a.m. for Chrissake.'

'Have you seen the paper?'

'You're joking! I hardly see daylight. Twelve-hour shifts, remember?'

'The law. They've changed the law.'

'What law? What *are* you talking about?'

'The adoption law. We can find our birth mothers. Shall we do it?'

'Look Sharon, I've just finished a twelve hour shift. I'm going to sleep like the dead. I'll talk to you tomorrow if I waken up.'

Mark put his arm around Steve's shoulder and said, 'Don't say things like that. You frighten me.'

'Like what?'

'Sleep like the dead.'

Sorry, but you know I am dead beat. Oh, sorry again.'

'Stop apologising and go to bed.'

When Mark followed him twenty minutes later, he noticed the dark rings under Steven's eyes and thought he couldn't continue to work these long hours.

'*Dring, dring.*'

The light was creeping under the curtains when Steve rolled over to pick up the bedside phone.

'Yeh?'

'So? You gonna do it? I don't think I can. I'm too scared. What do you think Mum would say? Dad wouldn't like it, would he?'

Steven sat up, stretched, yawned, and lay down again.

'Look Sharon, do you really think I decided in my sleep? It's been twenty years, longer for you. Tell you what. I'll come home at the weekend, and we'll talk about it.'

Mark came into the bedroom and put a cup of tea on the bedside table.

'Drink this and cheer up. It may never happen.'

'It already has.'

'It can't be that bad.'

'Can't it? It started when I was born. My own mother didn't want me. She gave me away. Can you imagine? My own mother gave me away? What sort of mother does that? Was I ugly? Did I cry all night? What about my father? Does he know I exist? Do you think he wanted to give me away as well? Do you know what it feels like to know that your parents actually gave you away?'

'No, I don't. But I do know that you've no idea why you were given away and making up stupid stories won't help. Anyway they call it relinquishing these days. Some mothers had their babies dragged from their arms while they screamed to keep them.'

'How would you know?'

'I saw it in that film *The Magdalene Sisters*. Look, Steve, now you are wanted. You've got Muriel who's a great Mum. She's like an oak tree.'

'What do you mean?'

'She is so firmly rooted and sturdy, nothing shakes her. Look how she accepted us when you came out. She was more upset about me giving up the church. And Jack, he's a pretty good dad – salt-of-the-earth kind o'bloke.'

'Yeh, right. That's why he never comes to see us. He hates me since I came out.'

'Give him time. He's from a different generation. He'll come round.'

'How much time does he need? It might be too late.'

'Stop whingeing and feeling sorry for yourself. You've also got two great sisters. Don't forget that they are adopted too. You never hear them going on about their birth parents. They know how lucky they are to have Muriel and Jack.'

'Well, now there's this new law that might change. That's why Sharon rang. We can do it. We can all find out where we came from.'

Steve opened the front door of his parent's suburban semi.

'Hi Mum, it's me. Mark's here as well. We both got the weekend off.'

'I'll put the kettle on. Sounds important if you're both here. You two getting married or something?'

'Very funny. I wish.'

Steve put his arms round his mum and planted a kiss on top of her head. *Mark's right*, he thought. *She is sturdy.*

'Shall I call your dad?'

'Not yet. I don't think he'll want to hear this.'

'It's OK, Steve. I've seen the paper, and I've talked to Sharon. You know I've always said that if you want to find your birth mother that's OK. I'll even help.'

Mark came into the kitchen saying, 'I've parked the car. Oh good you've made tea. Let's have a cuppa before we get serious. Where's your dad?'

'He's in the garden. Sharon's already told Mum, and Dad won't be interested. We'll leave him to his plants. They don't answer back, and they pretty much turn out the way they look on the packet; if they don't, you can dig them up and throw them on the compost.'

'That sounds very bitter, Steven. You know your dad loves you. It's just that you're not – you and Mark – you're not quite what he expected, that's all.'

'Yes, well, that's all in the past now. Let's talk about the present or should I say the future?' said Mark the peace maker.

'Where's Sharon? I thought we were going to make this decision together.'

'Sharon's not coming. Something about a double shift. I think she's calmed down a bit and had second thoughts.'

Muriel stood up and said, 'I think we need more tea.'

Mark gave Steve a knowing look. 'Come on, Steve. It's like you told Sharon. There's no rush. It's been twenty years. Why not give it time?'

Steven stood up and looked through the kitchen window into the garden. He could see his dad messing about in the greenhouse. Nothing was right. He wished he'd never been born. He turned round and said through gritted teeth, 'You know damn well time is one thing I haven't got.'

He went out slamming the back door. His dad looked up and said, 'Hi Steve! Don't slam the door like that.'

But Steven didn't hear. He was already half way to the car. Mark, who had followed him, grabbed his arm and said, 'Hold on there. I'm here for you, Steve. Come back and talk to Muriel. No good upsetting everybody about this.'

Steve's eyes brimmed with tears. 'That's the trouble. No matter what I do, I upset people. From the time I was born till... It'll be better for everybody when I'm dead.'

Mark flung both arms round Steven and said in a whisper, 'Don't you think you'd better tell your mum about the result of the AIDS test?'

'I can't. I just can't. She doesn't deserve it.'

'Neither do you or I, come to that. I know it's tough, but it's got to be done.'

They walked back to the kitchen and sat down.

'What was all that about? I've made some more tea,' said Muriel.

125

'I think a whiskey would be more appropriate,' said Steve.

'There's a bottle in the kitchen cabinet behind the electric mixer. Dad keeps it there for 'medicinal' purposes. Would you get it, Mark? I'll get the glasses.'

'Don't get one for me, Mark,' said Muriel. 'I don't drink at this time of day.'

'You will when you've heard what I have to tell you. Come and sit down, Mum.'

Steve placed three glasses on the table, and Mark poured out the whiskey.

'Mum, we both had an AIDS test some months ago. Mark's result was good. But, but I—'

'But yours wasn't.'

'No, it wasn't. It was the worst result one can get. I've got AIDS. I'm not just HIV positive. I've got full-blown AIDS.'

Just then Jack came in from the garden. 'What's this? Drinking in the day? I knew moving to London and working in a bar could lead to no good.'

'Sit down, Jack. You might want to join us when you hear what Steven has just told me.'

'Nothing to make me want to drink whiskey at this hour.'

'Jack, sit down and listen for once,' said Muriel in her 'listen or else' voice.

Jack sat and silently waited for an explanation.

'I think you two had better leave. I'll tell your father.'

'But Mum, what about you?'

'Do as I ask, please. I'll ring you.'

They left, and Muriel broke the news which was breaking her heart. She knew what it meant. She knew there was no cure. That her darling boy was going to suffer and die. And she would have to pretend that he was dying from something else. Cancer maybe.

Jack was walking up and down the kitchen shouting now.

'Well, it's not my fault he's gay. It's that bloody birth family he came from. It's not me, Muriel. It's not me.'

'Shut up, Jack. Can't you see? No matter what he is or what he does he's my son and he's going to die. Jack, he's going to die. There's no fault. There's no blame. He's been such a lovely son. What am I going to do, Jack? I need you. This is the time I need you. And he will need me.'

'Well, maybe he won't. Isn't he talking about finding his real mother? Maybe he needs her.'

'That's a really cruel thing to say. I'm his real mother. He might search for his birth mother now. Do you think he'll do it? What on earth will he say to her if he finds her? I'm your son and I'm dying of AIDS?'

Chapter Ten

Finders Weepers

Guilty Forty Years Later

I see
The tiny fingers and toes
The blue eyes and smudge of a nose.
I remember.
I hear
Breaths, murmurs and sighs
As he wriggles, stretches, then cries.
In my nightmares.
I feel
The ache, pain and sorrow
It'll be the same tomorrow.
I am sad
I know
He was born from my sin
With his hardly there hair and peach soft skin.
Of course I am guilty

[Jean Wild]

4 November 2004

Janet: 'I said I have some *sad* news. I left a message to say that I have some *sad* news. I hoped you'd hear that and be prepared.'

Me: 'No, no. I only heard news.'

Janet: 'I have some sad news. Simon died eleven years ago.'

Of course I cried.

Me: 'Eleven years ago?'

Janet: 'Yes, in 1993 on 26 April, a month...'

Me: 'A month after his birthday, I know. How? Was he ill? Did he have an acc—?'

Janet, 'AIDS. He died of AIDS.'

Louder sobs. *This isn't happening. I'm not here. It's a nightmare. It's not true.*

Me: 'Was he gay?'

Janet: 'Yes. His parents found that very difficult to cope with. They were – are – very religious.'

Me, 'Yes, I know they were Sunday school teachers – at least his mother was.'

Me: 'But it didn't—'

Janet: 'Affect their relationship? No. He had a very happy life. His mother rang me this morning. She must have phoned as soon as she received the letter. She was very upset. She was crying. I didn't want to ask too many questions. I didn't want to intrude, but I asked her if she had ever thought that you may one day try to find Simon. She said that she had never ever thought about it.'

Long silence.

Janet: 'She said he had a happy life.'

Me: 'That's good to know.'

Janet: 'She says she'll send some photographs.'

Me: 'I'd really like that.'

I do want to intrude. I want to know. Surely I have a right to know. I am, was, his mother too. He was my son as well. I missed his infancy, I didn't watch him go to school for the first time or complain about his teenage music. I didn't give him away because I didn't want him. I gave him away so that he would be safe.

I ran into Bill's arms and sobbed, 'He's dead. Simon's dead.'

We – Bill and I – went to a concert on Sunday afternoon. In the middle I had this longing to hold Simon in my arms, to have been there to take away his pain. I would have suffered his pain for him. How did he die? Where did he die? Where is he now?

14 November 2004

Yesterday I cried long and hard and could not stop. And today I am writing because I still can't stop crying. I wake up crying. I cry anywhere and everywhere. Thirty-nine years ago I had stopped myself from crying, and now the underground lakes of tears are making my head burst.

And still no video of *The Other Mother*. The title is very apt now. If only Simon's mum will accept me as the other mother, we could help each other I am sure. I rang Social Services to talk to Anita about the video. After three calls I had a message to say that it was in the post. That was more than ten days ago, but it still hasn't arrived!!

20 November 2004

Each time I have shared my 'news' with a friend, I have heard of another loss or bereavement. It is amazing how, when one opens up, people can empathise because they have had similar bereavements. To date I have heard that Daniel, a near neighbour, has lost a son. Another friend Monica told me that her son *and* his wife committed suicide leaving two children. Bill's golfing partner Peter told me that his daughter died of a drug overdose on Xmas Day. Mary, when she was only sixteen, had a son that she gave up for adoption. If I'd known how to share my pain all those years ago, perhaps I would have found enough support to search for my son before he died.

23 November 2004

All week I had hopes and fears about the promised photos – hopes that they would arrive and fears that Simon's mum would change her mind. I don't know why I refer to her as Simon's mum so easily, but I feel that we both were/are his mother.

When I returned one day to pick up my messages, there was one from Janet to say that she had received the photos, that Simon's mum had included her address, and also that his older sister, who was also adopted, had included her phone number. Incredible news! I was so excited. So much to write. Have I mentioned that they changed his name?

I can't think of him by any other name. He will always be Simon to me.

One evening when I was out having a meal with some classmates and Stephanie, it felt like an opportune moment to tell them about Simon. I wanted to explain my absence from class, so I said, 'I will tell you my bad news and then we will change the subject.' And I did. Then Josie told her story. It happened again. I tell the truth and someone else discloses.

She said, 'When I was fourteen, I gave birth to a baby boy. He contracted pneumonia. A month later he died. I was so young. I had to work. My mother looked after him. I felt guilty.' She took a photo out of her wallet saying, 'That's all I have.'

I was reminded that I had not taken any photos of Simon when he was born. 'Why not?' I ask myself frequently. I am going to get some, now that he is dead.

I dislike the euphemism 'lost'. I think it is dishonest. The truth is we did lose our babies when they were adopted. We didn't know where they were. Now we find that they are dead they remain lost no longer. We know exactly where they are. Except that now I am reminded again that I have no knowledge of what has happened to my son since his death.

So, lost again!!

Laura from NPN phones. She tells me that she is going to Australia to meet her son whom she gave up for adoption. I tell her the story about the woman who had a son adopted in England and then emigrated to Australia. She was sitting in a pub one day talking to a young man who told her that he had been adopted. As they shared histories they realised that they were mother and son. What are the chances of that? About the same as me discovering that my son died of AIDS eleven years ago, I expect.

I hate that word 'closure'. I hate it more than ever now because Simon will never be a closure. My heart will always be open, and he will always be in my memory. I shall have my own ceremony and special place to remember him. But no matter where I am or what I doing he will remain a part of me. I have just realised I am talking about remembering and not forgetting. I can now remember his birthday and the date on which he died. I can remember my grandson Stuart's birthday and my granddaughter Lizzie's. No more amnesia hopefully. What will the postman bring today?

Bill asked me, 'Do you wish that you'd never tried to find Simon?'

Fleetingly it had passed through my mind. I wouldn't be suffering the grief that I am suffering now. But just as quickly I said, 'No, because otherwise I would have spent the rest of my life wondering, hoping, and fearing.'

Maybe today will be the start of my new journey – getting to know Simon posthumously.

24 November 2004

The postman brought lots. All the usual advertising mags, a bank statement, and a flimsy green form to say that there was a letter waiting for me at the post office. I read it over and over. I ring Janet and we compare the number on the receipt with the number on my slip of paper.

They match.

25 November 2004

It's a beautiful sunny day. It's autumn in all her glory. I pick up the letter from the post office, which takes two minutes. I go to the supermarket for shopping soya milk etc. The large envelope is on the front seat of the car. I have to get diesel. I'm thinking all the time, *When and where shall I open the envelope? Not on a car park. Not in a lay-by. I must do it properly. I want to be alone when I meet my son for the first time.* I fill up with fuel. *I know*, I think, *I'll go to Plemet and sit by the lake.* As I am driving the car begins to jump and judder as though there is air in the fuel. The envelope lies unopened.

The car continues to lurch forward. What can I do? I am scared. I do not want to break down on this road. There is no hard shoulder. No phone box. I take the Plemet turnoff. I miss the Centre Ville sign and take the one to the Etang (lake). *I'll sit by the lake and open the envelope there.* The car stops dead at the next junction. I switch on the flashers, and somehow, after repeated attempts, I manage to get the engine started again; it limps forward till I spot a lay-by and I park there. Check to see if the car will start again. No, it will not. The letter remains unopened.

Now, what do I do? I take papers from the glove compartment. I find the number to ring for assistance. Before ringing I try to find the name of the road. I run up and down in a blind panic looking for a sign. There isn't one. I stop a woman with a baby in a pram and ask her. She doesn't know. At least it's not raining. It's a beautiful day. I can't see a phone box either. Go back to car and use mobile. Woman answers and puts me on hold. Will the credit last? Woman returns and asks for my number. Greater panic. I cannot remember my number. I have to look it up in my diary. Thank God I've got it. Hands shake. It's taking too much time. Will the battery last? Find page at last. Give number. 'I'll ring you back,' she says. I walk up and down. The phone is on energy save and repeatedly turns itself off. And the envelope is still unopened. She rings back.

Je suis desolée, Madame Wainwright. *Vous n'avez pas la depanage. Vous avez seulement l'assurance pour l'accident.*'

'Quoi? J'ai pensé oui.'

'No, madame. *Je vous donnerai un numero de telephone d'un depanage mais vous devrez payer.*'

'D'accord. Je peux l'écrire.'

I ring the number. This time the woman who answers tells me that her husband is not there; but she will not take my number. She keeps leaving the phone, saying, '*Ne quittez pas*'. *Isn't that a song? Is this really happening? Am I in a musical?* Finally I hear a man's voice. I tell him where I am. Then I hear those words which are at that moment better than 'I love you': '*J'arrive.*'

Thank you, thank you, thank you, someone. I sit in the car, and I see the envelope. My hand goes to it. I can't wait any longer. Stupid thing to do but I open it and stare at the photos. Then take out a folded leaflet and read, 'A Celebration of the life of Stephen Daniels'. I open the leaflet and read, 'Order of Service'. It lists the music played at his funeral. I don't know it. I want to hear it. I read it over and over and over. There's a message to my son from his partner. There's a message to the world from my son. These are the only words I shall ever receive from him, and I have to share them with all the world. But such beautiful words.

*They say we come into this world with nothing
and we leave this world with nothing.
I found that to be untrue.
So I say, thank you for the lessons learned, both given and received.
Remember me as a corpse – then I will be dead.
Hold to your truth in life, I will be free – and I will live on.
It is a choice between the slothful grey lizard or the soaring eagle –
We are each capable of both –
The choice is ours.
For as we bring in lessons to give to others,
We also receive lessons to take out with us
Which is why I have chosen the spiritual path
And have grown.*

I sob. I see for the first time after thirty-nine years photographs of my own son whom I shall never hold. My arms ache to hold the little, smiling boy in the photos who looks just like his brothers. Oh how I want to know the handsome young man sitting on the rocks beside the unknown-to-me sea!

I read and re-read the order of service many times. I want to hear the music. I should have been there.

There is the address of his parents and a telephone number for one of his adopted sisters. I look at the photo of my son with his two adopted sisters. They all have monkeys on their shoulders. It must have been taken on the Rock of Gibraltar. Was that a special place for them? They look happy. A happy family.

I try to 'pull myself together'. I hate that phrase. What does it mean? Don't show your feelings? Pretend that nothing is wrong? Always be happy? I dried my eyes and kept a lookout for the breakdown man. He arrived and put my car onto his breakdown truck.

Later at home I do not want to talk. Can't talk. I show Bill the envelope. He reads the contents and cries. I do not want him to cry. I can't support him. I want him to support me. I'm drained.

28 November 2004

Over the years I have had a recurring dream that I had a baby and let it die because I had forgotten I it. Mostly I managed to save it.

Last night I dreamt I was bathing a baby in a large white sink. I was daydreaming, looking out of the window or something. I suddenly remembered that there was a baby in the water. The baby had sunk to the bottom and was completely covered in water. He was lifeless. I grabbed his tiny body and lifted him out of the water. I attempted to give him mouth-to-mouth resuscitation, but I could not remember how to do it. *Should I blow or suck?* Then I thought that his lungs must be full of water. I turned him over and rubbed his back so that the water could escape. I woke before knowing whether he lived or died.

It's like a waterfall. Out come the tears, the anger, the frustration. Here we go again.

I go with Stephanie to Josie's for tea. Her house is Brazilian bright. Orange, yellow, and red jostle in the sunlight. It's dazzling. It reflects the warmth of our friendship.

Stephanie imparts some earth-shattering news, which reduces the temperature to an icy chill. Raymond has hung himself. He was a fellow student in the French class. Raymond was the kindest, gentlest, warmest man I have ever known. He must have hidden all his sadness from us.

He was disabled in a road accident. He couldn't find employment. The final straw came when his wife asked for a divorce.

I leave Josie's and drive back home blinded by tears. I don't know who I am crying for, my son or Raymond.

I had planned to watch the video. Did I mention that it had arrived?

6 December 2004

Today I feel normal, whatever that is.

After receiving the photos I wrote a letter to Jack and Muriel.

Dear Jack and Muriel,

Thank you so much for sending me the photos of Stephen and the order of service of his funeral.

I can't begin to tell you how much your kindness means to me. Obviously I have hoped all these years since his adoption that he was living in a happy home and now I know.

As you can imagine it was devastating to discover what had happened but it is comforting to learn from the words in the service that he must have grown into an exceptional young man. I am sure that your care and guidance and love all contributed to the making of a son you must have been proud of.

Of course I would have liked to have met him but feel that this glimpse into his life has told me so much.

Thank you also for sending Sharon's phone number. I talked to her tonight on the phone. She sounds like a lovely woman. You must be proud of all your children.

I hope we can keep in touch.

Thanks again,

Sincerely yours,

Sarah Wainwright

17 December 2004

I wrote the above letter about ten days ago. I can't remember the order of things but I remember the feelings. I rang Simon's sister who was speechless at first but then we had a long talk. She told me quite a lot and I talked about her mother. She said that she had tried to find her but some days she wanted to and other days she didn't.

Sharon told me that Simon's partner was called Mark Johnson. She said that he lived in Brixton. Or maybe they lived in Brixton. She's not sure whether he still lives there or not. She told me that Simon had wanted to find me. I found it difficult to talk about him using his other name. Sharon knew that I had called him Simon. How did they know that? If he knew his name then he would have been able to find me easily. Maybe he did find where I lived. Who knows what he found? Anyway he didn't make contact. I wonder who wrote that anonymous letter to David. Could it have been Simon himself? I don't know the date. Is this a dangerous corner?

I have been playing Tom Robinson, singing 'Glad to be Gay' and 'Dead All Dead'. Was his band called Sad Café? I also play a lot of Freddie Mercury lately. I have lots of him on video.

All in all I've had a few bad days.

19 December 2004

I feel a sense of total hopelessness.

Dead and gone,
I know not where,
Casket or coffin?
It's too hard to bear.
Death is so final
If only I'd known
My son as a child,
Or adult full-grown.

Not as a child
Nor as a man
Now I know
I never can
Hollow and empty
How I am sighing
to hold my own son
As he lay dying.

I feel cheated. I was given hope. He became real. I became real. Hope of finding my son. No more secrets. Now nothing. No hope. What is life if it is without hope? Is it really living? I don't believe in life after death. The only life we have is here and now. At sixty-four it's hard to invest in a future without hope.

I do not want to attend a funeral service in a church. I do respect other people's beliefs. I understand that some people may be comforted by their religion. But why do they not respect my beliefs? A church service only makes me angry. I do not believe in God.

I shall have a ceremony to say good-bye to Simon when I have lived with him in my mind as a child, a teenager, a young man, and an adult. I will be satisfied with a few glimpses of his life, something to carry in my heart. The alternative is to bury him as a baby, and I can't do that.

I have three losses to deal with:

I lost my baby.

I lost his living.

I lost his dying.

Losing the dying is the hardest to bear.

Can I ask for a death certificate to put with his birth certificate?

14 January 2005

Last Wednesday when I went in from the garden after planting hydrangeas I found a message on the answerphone from Muriel saying that she would ring me again. I was too scared to ring her. Could I talk about my own son to the woman who had raised him when I had given him away? I was feeling the loss of Jasper, my cat, who had died in the first week of January. I could hardly say, 'I'm upset because my cat has just died'. It doesn't compare with the fact that 'we' want to talk about our mutual son who died of AIDS, does it? How can someone who has given away a baby cry over a dead cat? Is it displaced grief?

Thursday I watch a TV programme about adoption and wish again that I had photos of Simon when he was a baby. I remember why I didn't even think about taking photos of him. Imagine what would have happened if my husband had found photos of my baby who was not his son. Proof of my adultery and worthlessness.

Friday evening Muriel rings again. She left another message. I had turned off the ringer. God knows why? What should I do? I have to ring. I am terrified. I ring.

Stilted conversation. She sounded kind. We both controlled our feelings and talked almost matter-of-factly. She talked about her grandchildren who are twins. I think she said that their mother was Susan, her younger daughter. She said that Sharon, her older daughter, had a son of twenty-one.

I told her that I had watched a video about adoption and that so many mothers had photos of their babies. I never had a baby photo of Simon. I always regret not having taken a photo.

'Do you think you could send me a baby photo?' I dared to ask.

She said she would. She told me that Simon had had a speech impediment but that after speech therapy it was sorted out. Apparently he confused sh, ch, and th. Susan, the younger sister, had copied, and they went through the same remedial process. I asked her where he had worked, and she said, 'Covent Garden Opera House'.

'Really? The Opera House?'

'Only in the bar,' she said.

'Was he interested in opera?'

'Not especially. He didn't dislike it, but he loved London. I remember walking through the West End with him and how he had stopped with arms outspread and said, 'Look at all this. Isn't it great?'

I asked her about his partner Mark Johnson.

'I was in contact until last year, but since then nothing. I have written to all the addresses I know, but he's a bit of a gypsy. I'm afraid he probably has AIDS, and he doesn't want me to know.'

'I wouldn't think that he would get it now,' I said. 'We know how to avoid it now.'

'Yes, but they are so careless.'

'It was difficult when he died, you know. Back then. We couldn't talk about AIDS. It was shameful. We told people he died of cancer.'

'That must have been very hard for you.'

'They were spiritualists, you know. Mark said that there were eight souls waiting for him when he died.'

'Did he die in a hospice?'

'No, he died at home surrounded by his friends and his carers.'

'Were you with him?'

'No, I wasn't.'

And she told me how she had gone to London to his flat, and he had been looking out of the window. She said, 'He looked so ill I hardly recognised him.'

'He found you,' she said.

My heart stopped. There was a long silence.

'What? What do you mean?' I said. 'He found me but didn't make himself known?'

'Yes. His friends talked him out of it. They said that he couldn't say, "Hi I'm your son and I've got AIDS".'

In my head I was screaming, *BUT HE COULD HAVE. HE COULD HAVE.* Now that is something that I have to live with.

I have so many questions.

When did he find me?

How much did he find out about me?

Did he know that he had two brothers?

Did he want to meet his father?

Now I feel that I can ask some questions and maybe get some answers.

16 January 2005

I've read all the books on grief and loss and mourning, but none of them speak to my condition.

Advice like 'pause and reflect on the memories of the person you loved' is inappropriate and painful to me.

18 January 2005

I have just been reading an entry in this journal from 2001. It seems that I put my name on the Adoption Register that year. It had taken me ten years from my discovery that there was such a thing to actually registering. Two pages before that entry there was at the top of the page, 'HE MIGHT BE DEAD. THAT'S WHY HE HASN'T CONTACTED ME'. When I wrote it I had thought that the idea was outrageous. But, *he was dead*.

24 February 2005

Last night I dreamt that I was lost in a muddy terrain. Stuart, my grandson, was ahead of me. He found his way to a well-lit, warm building, but I almost fell over a cliff. I managed to roll over to a safer path. I did reach the building, but I lost the parcel that I had been carrying. It was a shopping bag or a rucksack. I also dreamt that a group of mothers were talking to a group of young women about childbirth. One woman said that she thought that her swollen abdomen, which was covered in purple veins like a road map, was beautiful. I said that I didn't think mine was. I said that I thought it was ugly and that childbirth was excruciatingly painful. Then one of the women said that she didn't want to go through that pain. I said, 'But look what you will have at the end – a tiny human being, a person. The other mothers thought that I should not have said that it was painful. Then I felt guilty and thought that maybe they were right. I felt sorry for the girls. They looked afraid and confused.

25 February 2005

Woke very early crying as usual. I am very frightened and sad. Just when I thought I'd learned the trick of life, life tricked me and slapped me in the face.

'It's not what happens to you, it's the way you react to what happens to you.' How many times have I read this?

I do not know how to react.

Lately I've been very angry. All the books say that one of the stages of grieving is anger. I hate to think of myself as a text-book case, but I also know that I am no different from anyone else and that life goes on even though his doesn't. The world has been turning for millions of years and I am a speck. But just how does my life go on? Miserably. That is the exact word, miserably. I see nor feel no joy now. Everything is heavy and grey and leaden.

Everyday I go to the letterbox expecting to find an envelope with a photo of my baby. I do not know what to do except lie in bed and cry.

Everybody has different advice. Sylvia thinks I should just get on with life as though nothing has happened. Tricia wants me to rush around trying to contact everybody Simon ever knew and even invite his family over here. Pam is supposed to be trained in every kind of counselling and therapy devised but none of her comments ease my pain. Rachael makes subtle suggestions about moving forward with regard to the memorial I want to create. What no one seems to realise is that I have to deal with this in my own way. 'Memorial' is not the correct word. I have no memories so how can it be a memorial? I have a memory of pain, of the nine months of labour and a week of sheer agony knowing that the baby I was feeding was not coming home with me and I would never see him again. Then years of torture and then the search which lead to the knowledge of his death. I can't, do not want to create a memorial to agony, pain, and torment. What can I do? Do I have to return to forcefully forgetting again? As I write this the tears flow again uncontrollably. Will they ever stop?

I can do what I did when Simon was born and adopted. I could use mind over matter and make myself forget again. I do not know what else to do. I cannot function.

Does it have to get worse before it gets better? Will it get better? They say, I've said it myself: 'You never get over the death of a child.' My child has died twice. And I never even knew him. I do not know where his ashes are. I did not go to his funeral. He did not know me. Why was I born?

8 March 2005

I've waited two months for the photo, thinking every day that today it would come. One day the letterbox blew away and lots of letters were scattered all over the field. I found four or five letters. I want to ring Muriel to find out if she has posted it and it has been blown away, but I am too scared. What if she doesn't want to send me a photo or even talk to me again? Even worse, what if she sent me one and now it is lost? It would be like losing him all over again. Maybe I should call my story 'Losing Simon' not 'Searching for Simon'. I keep on searching, but all I ever seem to get are more disappointments.

19 May 2005

The garden I tried to make is a disaster. None of the bulbs or seeds have grown. All the wood I was hoping to sculpt repeatedly becomes overgrown with grass, nettles, and brambles. The pergola I bought, carefully stained, and treated won't fit together, and I do not know how to stand it up.

One positive step I took was to find the Compassionate Friends website which has proved to be such a comfort, although I don't feel that I fit in there either. Am I a fraud? Do I really have the right to grieve for the son I gave away? Is there anyone in the world who can understand? Simon, oh Simon, if you can hear me... But why should you ever want to listen to me? What did you find when you traced me? Did you find where I lived? Did you find out where I worked? Did you watch me? Did you see me? Why, oh why, didn't you come and give me a big hug?

I can hear a cuckoo. I hear it every morning and every evening. All I can think about is that it lays its eggs in other birds' nests. The baby cuckoo pushes all the other eggs out of the nest, and the hosts have to feed the cuckoo. A kind of adoption. Am I a cuckoo? Was my baby a cuckoo?

I wrote ages ago to Simon's mother to ask her if she had sent a photo and explained about the letterbox, but I have had no reply. What is she afraid of? I can't take him away now that he is dead. Is she afraid that I will steal her memories? I can't do that. Her memories are her memories. Doesn't she know the pain I'm in? I suppose that she is thinking, 'Well you shouldn't have given him away, should you?' And there is always the added guilt that I was not a young unmarried mother. I was a married woman who had an affair. 'Affair'! That's rich.

17 June [2005]

I feel guilty because I feel such loss. How can I talk about grieving for a son that I gave away when so many mothers are grieving for stillborn babies or babies of three months of age or six months or two years or six years? I can hear them all saying, 'Well, you shouldn't have given him away.' Of course I shouldn't have, but I did and now he's dead. I'm in a club for one.

15 July 2005

I tried to paint a frame to put Simon's photo in, but it wasn't successful. I thought I would hang it on the wall, then when someone asks about it, I can say, 'That's my son – my youngest son who died from AIDS.' But I didn't.

I am becoming reluctant to talk about Simon again. It's like tearing off the scab again. Why do it?

Just when I had given up hope of ever receiving the photos, I found a letter in the box with an English postmark. I opened the envelope and voila! THE BABY PHOTOS! I couldn't believe it. I burst into tears. There was a short chatty letter included as though it had only been a couple of weeks since they had been promised, not six months. I thought at least after my letter about the box blowing away she would have replied. I wonder if she realises how much they mean to me. She was quite flippant about it.

Dear Sarah,

So sorry it has taken me so long to write. I just don't know where the time goes. We went to Torquay, and tomorrow we are going to Epsom to see Susan and the twins. On Wednesday I am going to prison. No not to stay! The Mothers Union runs a crèche for the children of visitors; then in the evening I am going to the 80th birthday celebration of another M.U. So this is how the time goes.

The photos are not blowing around France, although I can imagine Stephen thinking it quite a hoot if he was.

Here are the photos. Hope you are keeping well,

Yours sincerely

Muriel

I feel as though it is a letter that I can reply to so that I can keep in touch.

I rang Bill straight away. He was very empathetic as always. I do not want to tell anyone else.

One of the topics for discussion on TCF (The Compassionate Friends) website lately has been about not including all our children in our conversation about our children. For example, when asked how many children do you have? I always reply, 'Two'. I could never say, 'Three, but I gave one up for adoption'. Recently I wanted to say, 'Three, but my youngest son died'. I can't cope with the explanation that I anticipate would inevitably have to follow. It's taken me a few years to feel comfortable saying, 'My son Simon.' he feels more like a real person every day. I can even bring a picture of him into my mind now that I have the photos.

29 July 2005

I no longer feel that I belong on TCF website.

How can I talk to other women who have had stillbirths or women whose baby of one week or three months or child of ten or teenager or newly married who...?

I GAVE MY BABY AWAY. I GAVE MY BABY AWAY.

I wrote to Muriel and Fred.

Dear Muriel,

Thank you for sending me the baby photos. I can't tell you how much they mean to me. I have so little to remember him by.

They look like originals. If you would like them back, let me know and I will make copies.

I know what you mean about time flying.

I hope you get to see your grandchildren often. They must be a real delight for you.

Please keep in touch when you feel able.

Thank you again,

Best Wishes

Sarah

I feel like a stupid little girl. Begging, not daring, whispering. Why? Why can't I speak up and say what *I* need? Why can't I ask for what I want? Where did the treading carefully get me? Where did doing as someone else said get me? Nowhere, nowhere.

MY SON IS DEAD.

Dear Simon,

What can a mother say to a son she gave away? Only platitudes come to my pen: 'I did it for you'; 'It was for the best.' This is only partly true. I also did it for myself, which turned out not so good for me. I hope it was better for you.

I know I should not have had an affair when I was married and already had two sons. But if I hadn't, you wouldn't have been born.

Muriel told me that you found me. Why, oh why, did you not come to me and say, 'I am your son.' I would have thrown my arms around you and hugged you and begged your forgiveness. I would have wanted to know all about you. I read your words in the funeral service, and from those words I know it would have been a privilege to know you. It hurts so much having a vision of you searching and finding me. I gave birth to you. I should have been there for you when you were ill. If you had to die, you should have died in my arms.

If there is a heaven, I know that you are there. You are at peace, free from pain and free from discrimination.

This week the law has changed, and gay people can marry – single sex marriages. Would you have married? I would have been so proud to have been at your wedding.

I want to believe in life after death so that I can meet you, but I can't. I really can't believe it.

Perhaps I'll write again. I know you can't write back. Why didn't you write me a letter all those years ago? So many questions and never any answers.

Your very loving,

Birth Mum

22 December 2005

I received a Xmas card signed, 'Best wishes, Muriel and Jack'. I am determined to write and ask if I can visit. I have a feeling that Muriel would like to meet me. Everybody is telling me to be careful about other people's feelings and how I should be grateful that his parents are communicating with me. I feel like an unworthy beggar. I have feelings too, damn it. Haven't I been the one who has suffered the most? Am I not the one who missed my son's life and death? Muriel and Jack had him. He loved them. They loved him. Surely they can't refuse to share a few of their memories with me. I am/was his mother.

The card, by the way, was a picture of the Virgin Mary holding Baby Jesus!!

31 January 2006

(England in Tesco's. Waiting for a friend.)

I did write to Muriel and Jack to ask them if I could meet them. I thought that Muriel would be happy to talk to me about our 'mutual' son. As things turned out I booked a ferry after Xmas and wrote to them just before I left. I gave them the address and phone number of the place where I would be staying but till today I heard nothing. This morning I suddenly decided that it was now or never so I rang directory enquiries for their number and I rang. Jack answered. I was scared but said, 'It's Sarah Wainwright speaking. Did you get my letter?'

'Er, yes we did.'

'What do you think? How do you feel about it?'

'I'll pass you to my wife.'

A very quiet voice said, 'Hello.'

I repeated my question, 'Did you get my letter?'

'Yes.'

'What do you feel about it? Would you like to meet?'

'Yes.'

'When? Which day?'

'I'm rather busy. I only have Friday free.'

'Friday is fine. Is your place difficult to find or would you like to meet somewhere neutral?'

'I thought we could meet in Birmingham. Is that OK? Marks & Spencers. Do you know where that is?'

'No but I can find it.'

'There's a precinct and an open area for food.'

'I'll find it. How will we recognise each other?'

Long silence. I am thinking that wearing flowers would be stupid. Inappropriate.

She says, 'I'll wear my brown coat, no jacket. It's a what's-it-called?'

I say, 'Fleece?'

She says, 'Yes, that's it. I'll wear my brown fleece.'

'I'll be wearing my padded coat. It looks like a quilt. It's black and it's got purple trimmings.'

'What time?'

'Twelve o'clock.'

'OK. I'll see you on Friday at twelve o'clock in Marks & Spencers in Birmingham.'

I put the phone down. I'm in a turmoil. *How the hell am I going to drive into and out of Birmingham? On a Friday too!* I look at a map and think about parking outside and going in on the train. It looks complicated. I consider going from here by train. But I have to drive down to London after, and it would be too late. Then I lose my car keys, and after the first panic dies down I realise that I can change things if I have to.

Arrangements are not carved in stone. I have to stop turning myself inside out to fit in with other people. So when I find my car keys, I do just that. I ring Muriel and ask if she could change the day to Thursday. She says no, she has an appointment on Thursday. I tell her that I am not happy about driving into Birmingham and that I have to come by car as I will be driving to my sons in London after our meeting.

'Can we meet somewhere else? Somewhere easier with less traffic?'

She says, 'We can meet in Halesowen. Do you know where that is?'

'I've got a map. I can find it. Is there a shopping centre or something that is easy to find?'

'Yes, there's a precinct called The Bow Centre.'

'Is there a café we can meet in?'

'Yes, it's an open space in the middle.'

'Fine. I'll follow the signs for the town centre and then find the precinct.'

'Look forward to meeting you on Friday.'

Chapter Eleven
Mothers' Meeting

Wearing her black quilted coat with the purple trims she set out early. She knew that the journey would normally only take a couple of hours, but the last thing she wanted was to be late. She had sat on the M6 in endless traffic jams in the past, and although she had studied the map for hours she was still nervous about finding the shopping centre in a strange town sixty miles away. She touched the map beside her on the passenger seat and thought, *Thank God I changed the venue from the middle of Birmingham to a town on the outskirts*. She knew she was a good map reader, but driving in Birmingham any day of the week would be difficult and on a Friday it would be madness.

As she pulled up at the next traffic light her hand strayed to the map and her instructions on the passenger seat. It calmed her churning stomach a little to concentrate on the journey and not the meeting, but she still drummed the steering wheel impatiently. When the lights changed, she let out the accelerator too quickly, kangarooed forward, and stalled like a learner. Restarting the engine quickly, she moved off more carefully. She didn't want to die on the way. What irony would that be!

Sixty miles away in a suburban semi another woman looked in the hall mirror as she zipped up her brown fleece; she wondered if her scarf matched and why she was bothered. She was not normally concerned about how she looked. She was not even sure why she was going. Was it curiosity? Try as she might, she couldn't think of one good reason to be going. She could think of lots of reasons why she shouldn't go, and yet she zipped up her fleece, tied on the scarf, put on a hat, and left the house. She walked to the bus stop as though being drawn by an invisible thread. Waiting for the bus, she realised that she was going to arrive too early. Oh well, she could do some shopping first. After all they were meeting in a shopping precinct. She wondered why the meeting had been changed from Birmingham city centre. The city centre would have been more anonymous for her. She would have liked a day out in the city. On the familiar journey to town, she wrote a list to keep her mind off her churning stomach. If anybody saw her, they would just think that she was going shopping.

She hated motorway driving, and the M6 was the worst. The quilted coat had been a mistake. It was too long and it got in the way of the gear lever. Why had she said that she would wear it? Yes, well, why had she done and said a lot of things much worse? She saw the exit sign she was looking for and noticed that she was gripping the steering wheel so tightly her knuckles had turned white and she was getting pins and needles. She must relax. Easier said than done. The directions she had written down from the phone call were matching well with the signposts, and she soon found herself stopping in a multi-storey car park. She looked at her watch. Eleven o'clock. Oh no! Now she was too early. She walked slowly towards the shopping centre, which was easy to see from a distance. It used to be churches that overlooked the towns. Now it was the neon lights of the temple of the new religion of shopping. She stopped in front of a florist's and, as if guided by external forces, bought a bouquet of flowers.

Entering the centre she immediately saw the sign for the café. It was in the middle surrounded by market stalls. Wanting to kill time, she idly glanced at the one selling second-hand books. Her hand fell on a tiny, beautifully bound copy of poetry by Thomas Hardy. She bought it and also a cup of coffee. She found a well-placed table so that she could easily be seen. She sat down to drink her coffee and opened the book of poems. She glanced frequently at the large clock on the wall. Half an hour to go.

As she got off the bus she thought it might seem odd if she turned up with bags of shopping. But, what the hell, she couldn't sit in the café for an hour. Somebody would recognise her and ask to join her or—or—or anything. So she bought an odd variety of items because she didn't really need anything. Strolling as slowly as she could around the supermarket, she took things absent-mindedly from the shelves. Her only concern was that the things should be light enough for her to carry. She normally came shopping with Jack in the car. Oh my God, he would wonder why she had bought all this stuff when she had come by bus and was supposed to be visiting a friend. Suddenly remembering that she had left a roll of film at the chemist's, she searched for the ticket in her purse. Yes, there it was. So she picked up the photos and thought what a brilliant idea that she could look at them in the café. She chose a table where she would easily be visible, looked at the clock, and thought, *Fifteen minutes to go.* There was a long queue at the counter. She wondered whether to join it.

****

The two women sat in the café on adjacent tables. Strangely they were aware of each other although neither of them appeared to be. One was dressed in a black full-length quilted coat with a purple collar. She was reading a tiny volume of poetry; a bunch of flowers lay on the floor beside her. The other, who was wearing a brown fleece, was arranging two bags of shopping. She placed them on separate chairs to save two seats.

Quilted Coat continued reading the book of poetry which she had bought only minutes before from a second-hand stall nearby.

Brown Fleece left her bags knowing that she could keep an eye on them, and she joined the long queue at the counter.

Quilted Coat now glanced along the queue taking in the brown fleece and knew that it was she.

Brown Fleece glanced around the tables taking in the quilted coat and knew that it was she.

Quilted Coat read a line in a poem. 'Whose is the child you are like to bear?...' ('Tramp-woman's Tragedy').

Christ, she thought, *is it my life story?* Quickly she turned to another page and read, 'Here's physic for untimely fruit...' ('Sunday Morning Tragedy'). She snapped the book shut and wondered if she had imagined the words. She must concentrate on today and looked to see if the queue had lessened.

The tension built up in both of them. They tried to prepare first word greetings. None seemed to come. They avoided each other's furtive looks and thought harder. They had both said to themselves, 'It must be her. She's wearing what she said she would.'

Finally just as Brown Fleece is picking up her coffee Quilted Coat rushes over to her and whispers, 'Muriel?'

'Yes,' Muriel replies.

Quilted Coat inappropriately kisses her on the cheek then points to her table.

Muriel says, 'Sarah, I've saved a table for us over where the shopping bags are.'

The practicalities solve the problem of the opening lines, and the use of first names eases some of the tension. They arrange themselves comfortably. An awkward silence follows. They wonder how to break it and hope that there wouldn't be too many of them.

Muriel takes out the packet of photos.

'I've just picked them up. They're photos of our Susan's twins. We saw them just before Xmas.'

Sarah thinks, *How clever of her to bring something to focus on. Photos. Always good icebreakers. She makes what she thinks are the right noises. It's like a script.*

'How old are they? Twins? You must be thrilled. They are alike. Can you tell them apart? Who do they look like?'

And they both know that this is not why they are here.

Muriel blurts out, 'Now, what are all these questions that you want to ask me?'

And Sarah, who had planned to write a list but hadn't, is taken aback.

After a few seconds she begins, 'Er... well, er... I wonder, you know, he found me you said on the phone. When did he find me?'

Muriel takes what seems to Sarah a long time and thinks,

How can you not remember? Then she rebukes herself for this criticism comparing it to her own past behaviour.

At last Muriel says, 'Well, he was ill for about a year, and it was when he first became ill. So it would have been about ninety-two.'

Sarah is too afraid to say, 'What did he find out about me?' But she asks,

'Do you know why he didn't make himself known to me?'

'He wanted to, but his friends said you can't say, "Hello, I'm your son, and, by the way, I've got AIDS".'

Sarah pales and inside she is screaming, *BUT HE COULD HAVE. HE COULD HAVE. HE COULD HAVE.* She casts her mind back and remembers that her father died in January ninety-two and her best friend later the same year. But that made it worse. No matter what was going on, it would have been the happiest day of her life if he had knocked on the door and said, 'Hi, I'm Simon.' She would have said, 'Hi Simon, I'm your mother. I have been longing to meet you.'

'It was hard for us too, you know.'

Muriel's words cut into Sarah's thoughts and she looks up and tries to focus her attention.

'Of course it must have been. No one expects their children to die before them.'

'It was more than that, you know. At that time we were ashamed to tell the truth. We told people that he died from cancer.'

Their eyes meet, and they both understand the depth of their mutual grief.

Sarah looks away and tries hard to remember the list which she hadn't written down.

'I think you said that Mark, his partner, had his ashes.'

'Yes,' says Muriel.

'Doesn't that—aren't you—wouldn't you—? I believe that most crematoriums have a book in which all names are written. They turn the page over every day, and you can go and read the deceased's name...'

'All that doesn't bother me – cemeteries, graves, ashes. That's not how I remember people.'

Sarah thinks, *Well, it's OK for you. You have memories. I'd like something concrete.* But instead she says, 'I know what you mean. I never go to the crematorium where my parents are. I have paintings of them to remember them by.'

Muriel says, 'He believed in reincarnation, you know.'

'Yes, I gathered as much from the funeral service that you sent me,' Sarah replies.

Muriel goes on, 'I said to him one day when he was talking about it, "Well, if you do come back, make sure that it's to someone who can keep you next time".'

And then she asks, 'Do you feel guilty?'

Sarah replies honestly, 'No, not that he was adopted because he obviously went to a lovely family' (Muriel smiles, a bit smugly, Sarah thinks) 'but that he was conceived because I had an affair.' (Sarah thinks, also smugly, *But if he hadn't been, you wouldn't have enjoyed him.*)

'One thing I've found since you contacted me. I can talk about his dying without getting upset.'

Sarah notices that, even so, she almost cries now. She recognises the effort of talking and the tell-tale twitching of the mouth, which really wants to cry, and the squeezing of the eyes, which want to shed tears.

'Well, almost,' she adds.

'Sharon brought me a photo of him and me together. And I thought, "I can't live with that. I'll hide it in the bedroom." But Sharon put it up in the living room, and I've got used to it now.'

Sarah thinks, *I can never have a photo of him and me together.*

'One thing that might help you... I've got a vase that I put flowers in on his birthday and Xmas and so on,' Muriel says.

All Sarah's elaborate plans for a secret garden now seem ridiculous, inappropriate, over the top. She remembers that she had nearly bought a huge set of rustic garden furniture, which included table and chairs under a pergola. She had also vaguely planned a sculpture park.

Sarah saw that Muriel had missed his birth but had had his twenty-seven years of life and his death. A simple vase of flowers enabled her to mourn and grieve. No matter what she, his birth mother, had planned, it had not helped her to come to terms with her grief. She'd lost him twice. There were too many lost possibilities and so much unfinished. There was too much aching and longing, too much unfulfilled. She had had his birth. She had missed his life and his death.

Perhaps between them they could bring his birth, life, and death together in a single flower vase.

Sarah picks up the flowers she bought and says, 'I brought these for you.'

'I'll put them in Simon's vase,' says Muriel.

Epilogue

Sitting on Simon's seat once more, I have just one more tale to tell. It is rather fantastic, but you know truth really is stranger than fiction.

The Best-laid Plans

(sometimes turn out even better than we hoped)

I was continuing with my life, not planning anything special, just treading water, I suppose. I sometimes thought that I would like to contact Mark. He and Simon cared for each other so deeply. This was clear from the words they wrote for the funeral service. I thought that maybe I could have some kind of relationship with Mark and perhaps through him learn a little more about my son. I had absolutely no idea how to go about finding him.

I only knew two concrete facts about Simon: he had worked in the bar at the Royal Opera House and lived with Mark in Brixton. But that was years ago, and the Opera House has since been completely renovated.

Then one day I received a letter from Muriel, Simon's adoptive mother, saying, and I quote her exactly, 'Your depression is contagious, and I can do without it.'

I wasn't depressed before I received the letter, but her words threw me into a deep depression. I asked friends if they found me depressive. I mulled it over. I went back over our conversation in that café – such a public place to have had such an intimate meeting. I slowly came to the conclusion that she was the one who was depressed. I composed many letters to her. Each one tried to point out to her that it was not me who was depressed but her. I had, after many years, faced reality and thrown off *my* depression. I had grieved and mourned my losses and learned that one never forgets death and loss but learns to live with it. I realised at that meeting that she still had some grieving to do. I thought that she was holding it back together with the anger she was afraid to acknowledge. Repressed feelings of anger and grief are two certain causes of depression. Of course I sent none of the letters. But I did throw off the effects of the letter. And I determined to do something about finding Mark.

I 'googled' the name Mark Johnson on the Internet. Thousands of Mark Johnsons came up. So, short of employing a private detective, I was bereft of ideas.

However, I found my hard-learned positivity again. I took myself in hand. I gave myself a good talking to and made a plan. I accepted the fact that I could never speak to anyone who had know my son. But I could go to the place where he had lived and worked. I would take a holiday in London. I would stay in a grand hotel. I would imagine that he was with me, and we would spend his birthday together. Hang the cost. I had missed over forty birthdays. We could have the time of our lives. Forty birthdays rolled into one. Why not? Just Simon and me. If I didn't have any memories, I would make some.

So I did just that. I went to London and stayed in a proper hotel – not a cheap hostel as I usually did. After breakfast I went to Brixton and walked the streets wondering where he could have lived. I went in and out of the shops thinking he probably bought his newspapers here and his food there and maybe he drank in that pub. After a while it felt like Simon was with me and we were walking hand in hand. I suggested taking a taxi to the West End and he agreed.

We dined well at lunch time in a five-star restaurant. All the time I was talking to Simon in my head. I hope it was all in my head. I don't think any of the words escaped. I asked him what he wanted to drink, and we shared a bottle of the finest champagne. He chose his favourite dishes from the menu. I almost ordered a birthday cake with forty candles to be brought to the table. But I didn't want to attract attention to myself. People would think I was a little crazy (I don't look forty) and sad (like those who celebrate their birthday alone in public). So no cake. We had such a good time together. Over the meal I explained everything to him, the circumstances of the adoption, and all about my new life in France. We decided that this would be the first of many birthday celebrations.

After lunch we took another taxi to Covent Garden. I told him that I had always loved the atmosphere there and that I had bought CDs of the string quartet that plays in the market café. He said he thought it had changed a lot since he was last there. We drank tea and had scones oozing with jam and cream in a rooftop café.

We walked over to the Opera House and decided to have a drink in the bar where he had worked. He said that it felt odd sitting there with his mother when his job had been behind the bar serving other people.

'Let's go really mad' I said, 'and go to the box office and take a box for the evening performance.'

He said,' But we don't know what it is.'

And I said, 'It doesn't matter.'

So we did. I mean, I did.

'The box is for four people, madam,' said the cashier. 'It is £185 each, and you have to buy all four places.'

'It's for two—sorry—I mean, one person. I am alone.'

'That will be £740 please, madam.'

Simon blanched at this and said, 'You really can't spend that much, Mum.'

I said, 'Of course I can. It's forty years worth of birthday presents.'

So we ordered interval drinks and bought a huge box of my favourite chocolates. We installed ourselves comfortably and waited for the curtain to rise on 'Madam Butterfly'. Well, it had to be that, didn't it? At least I thought it is in English.

During the interval there was a knock on the door, and a young man came in with the drinks that I had ordered.

I said, 'I prefer tea in the interval. It helps to keep me awake.'

He looked puzzled because I had ordered tea for two and I was obviously alone.

'Please join me,' I said quickly. 'I did order two cups.'

He was reluctant at first, but I pressed him, saying, 'Oh do indulge an old lady. You wouldn't refuse your grandmother, now, would you?'

He sat in Simon's chair, but I didn't say anything. He took his tea and stared me straight in the eye.

'D'you know, you remind me of someone. Are you a singer? I think I've met you before.'

'No, I am not a singer.'

'Did you used to have a season ticket? Your face is so familiar.'

'No, I have never been here before, and I have lived in France for the last five years. You must be confusing me with someone else.'

He left, looking puzzled. If I was younger, I would have thought that he was coming on to me – spinning me a line, as they say. Then the curtains opened again, and I remembered that I was with Simon. I concentrated on the opera. As the story unfolded I recalled the end. The agony of losing a child ripped at my heart all over again. I squeezed Simon's hand tightly and whispered, 'That's how I felt when I gave you away.'

As the final curtain came down he said, 'You didn't kill yourself like the woman in the opera.'

'No,' I said. 'I didn't kill myself because of my other two sons, but—'

'I'm glad,' he said.

'But part of me died.'

Then there was a knock on the door, and the same young man came in again.

'I am sorry to disturb you, but I've remembered who you remind me of.'

I started to say 'of whom you remind me' when he thrust a photo in my face.

'That's a young man. How can I remind you of a young man?'

Then I recognised the photo.

'I have the same photo. I keep it on my dressing table. That's my son Simon. How come you have a photo—you must be—are you Mark?'

So you see, miracles do happen. Every year I celebrate Simon's birthday by going to Brixton and the Royal Opera House. I *have* created that memorial garden, and I sit on Simon's seat to remember the happy times that I have created with him and of course the ones that Mark has provided me with and also the ones we have created together – Mark and I.

Jean Wild

Useful Addresses

N.P.N.
18 Bishops Way
Stradbroke
EYE
Suffolk
1P21 5JR
www.n-p-n.co.uk

AAA NORCAP
11Z Church Rd
Wheatly
Oxon
OX33 1LU
www.org.uk

About the Author

Jean Wild, now retired, has had a multitude of jobs which include teaching and desktop publishing. She calls herself 'Jill of all trades and mistress of none'. She writes, paints, dances, plays the clarinet for dancing and the piano for herself. Her latest and all consuming passion is gardening.

Being close to 70 she wanted to publish her experiences and thoughts on a number of women's issues, in particular adoption and depression. She is a woman of very strong beliefs and will always take action or speak out when faced with inequality or injustice. Perhaps for this reason she has been called judgmental.

The play she wrote in the 90's was performed in her home city in England and was well received.

She lives deep in the countryside of Brittany with her three cats and enjoys life to the full.

Printed in Great Britain
by Amazon